MENTAL HEALTH SURVIVAL GUIDE

For Individuals and Families of Indian Origin

GREESH C. SHARMA, Ph.D.

Vasudhaiva Kutumbakam is a Hindu belief meaning "the entire world is a family". In reality, biological or global family comes with its own conflicts, confusion, chaos, challenges, crisis, and cross-cultural distress.

To survive, maintain, sustain and thrive in the context of living amongst strangers, alien cultures, foreign lands and inter-racial, interethnic and inter-religious social milieus, one needs more than faith, intellect, money, professional excellence and family support.

Good mental health requires a strong foundation in spirituality, insight into one's emotional make up, clarity as to values/belief systems, skillful decision making and ultimately, the ability to balance between the pulls and pushes of myriad internal and external, predictable and unpredictable challenges.

A mentor, Guru, psychologist, wise counselor, or support group can save time, avert crisis, and prevent costly mistakes. Of course, the essence of life is happiness, and the purpose of psychotherapy is not just to cure mental problems but to facilitate happiness and growth.

Greesh C. Sharma, Ph.D.
1400 Heller Drive, Yardley, PA 19067
drgreesh@yahoo.com

ISBN 978-0-9886516-1-6

Contents

Foreword

According to research by the Pew Foundation, Indian Americans have the highest education level of any ethnic group within the United States. Two sitting Governors are of Indian descent and celebrities such as the journalist/physicians Drs. Sanjay Gupta and Atul Gawande, are well known to and respected by many Americans. In the popular mind, Indian Americans are the "model minority."

Yet, Dr. Greesh Sharma punctures the myth of the "model minority" with both an aerial and a grounded view of Indians in the United States & in the Western world. Despite financial and educational success, Asians/Indians face many problems, both within the United States and in other parts of the world. Indian immigrants have faced many hardships including deeply ingrained prejudices and micro-aggressions.

From the aerial perspective, Dr. Sharma provides a broad sweep of Indian history, culture, and customs. From the grounded standpoint, Dr. Sharma gives details of Indian customs that every mental health professional should know and presents informative case studies that illustrate these factors and conflicts. Dr. Sharma appreciates the complexity of clinical decision making which must consider gender, socio-economic status, and other factors as well as ethnic identity.

Dr. Sharma reviews the role of stigma, family customs and communication patterns, and the role of beliefs in the willingness to seek mental health treatment. Furthermore, Dr. Sharma reminds us that no culture, including Indian culture, is stagnant. Instead, Indian culture is changing under the influence of globalization, including Western notions of dress, manners, and consumerism.

Dr. Sharma is well equipped to present this picture. Not only is he a licensed clinical psychologist who has done extensive clinical work with Indian Americans, he also has traveled extensively to many parts of the world which have large Indian emigrant populations. This book provides essential information for mental health professionals who are involved in the treatment of Indian diaspora, as well as for Indian mental health consumers.

-    Samuel Knapp, Ed.D. ABPP.

Director, Professional Affairs, Pennsylvania Psychological Association, Member of the Asian American Psychological Association.

Preface

My fascination with human beings, their struggles, creativity and resilience in general has been in my awareness since childhood. Indians, in particular, have been a subject of curiosity and concern since my adolescence. Initially it was simply my visceral reaction after having read Indian history as a student and concluding that Indians were perpetually victimized by invaders; that foreign aggressors, after the end of Ashoka the Great Empire, practically rewrote the Indian history and altered Indian national character. I was always motivated to understand how tiny groups of Greeks, Turks, Kushans, Huns, Sakas Persians, and Muslim marauders from central Asia and elsewhere could come on a whim and raid the heartland of the country with no serious resistance, violent reactions, dire repercussions, guilt or shame. This process of India's cultural rape and the century's long history of Hindu holocaust evoked in me a very strong urge to understand and decipher what it is about Indians that draws them to tolerate victimization, accept subjugation, and opt for a modus operandi of non-violence and never ending apathy.

Indians' indifference and habitual failure to confront adversaries extends beyond any rational analysis. At the same time, I am fascinated as to what made the Mongols, British, Portuguese, and French so effective in subjugating and exploiting India and, in the process, abolishing a uniquely ancient mother of all civilizations.

The simplest explanation is that the Hindu belief system imposes the only option, i.e. non-reactivity, which implies neither taking charge nor controlling the situation and indirectly opting for apathy – in turn aiding and enabling alien adversaries. Such passivity has historically empowered aggressors. All invaders who came to India have claimed to be superior to Indians. Adversaries' self-righteous pragmatism allowed them to freely resort to use any means or tactics, ultimately enriching themselves through pirating and poaching knowledge, gold, spices or cheap labor. India's fate was sealed because of these unscrupulous and aggressive maneuvers.

This is a double-edged sword. If Hindus become like their adversaries then their civilization will cease to be spiritual, unique and enduring. Paradoxically, if Hindus do not respond to their adversaries in kind, and succumb to adversarial tactics of violence, proselytization and psychopathic maneuvers, their identity will become unrecognizable. This Hindu dilemma, a catch 22, is what has been the trap for the past

2000 years. Not challenging the alien adversaries has resulted in India's fragmentation and partitioning again and again while, at a human level, becoming traumatized. India continues to bleed and the threat of partition looms larger than ever with alien adversaries waiting for Indians to continue to disintegrate with regard to their mental health, personality and national character.

Jews have never stopped examining and reexamining the holocaust, but Indians have yet to learn to become even comfortable with talking about their historical traumas as a nation. This Indian detachment and cognitive dilemma has rarely been contemplated, examined critically or debated openly by Indians. It is my intention in this book to bring to light these important discussions so that they may begin to be transformed and healed.

Indian national atrophy has become synonymous with the national character. It is also used to fill the gap and buy time with the fantasy in mind that, someday, magic will happen and India will rise from the ashes. As inevitable as the Commercial globalization phenomenon is, it is digging the final grave of whatever little is left of Indian civilization and culture. Indian society has accepted defeat and concluded that whatever happens will be their national destiny. Those civilizations that allow existence by default and passivity usually end up being defined, controlled and enslaved by religious, political or militant terrorists.

These observations and conclusions have impelled me to explore the crescendos of Indian civilization and dynamics of the Indian National Character through the binoculars of clinical psychology and mental health. It is inevitable that the pursuit will not always be pleasant and conclusions may also point towards weaknesses as well as strengths. Unlike other cultures and civilizations, one thing uniquely stands out about India and Hindus, that the destination is nothing less than the wellbeing of the world, unconditional acceptance of all, and never controlling, contaminating, or manipulating others' identity, culture or way of life. This is the ultimate spirituality in the Indian character and makes non-violence the core of their existence

The Indian Diaspora Handbook explores the present as well as the past. It further seeks to understanding the historical and social context as to where one is coming from, and how one is managing the myriad variables interacting in the present. Indians' preferred coping mechanisms, as well as the strength and resilience Indians display, are all rooted to a large extent in the present (Time, Place & Person) and spiritual ideals, and significantly in their personal need for "freedom from it all".

What started out as simply an interest in Indian history later became a deliberate passion to feel, touch, hear, and experience the larger context called the Indian Diaspora. My choice to become a psychologist proved to be an ideal medium. It gave me opportunities to visit Indian Diaspora countries to offer mental health/addiction treatment service camps, give workshops and lectures and fifty years of private practice. Encounters with people of the Indian diaspora in different countries proved to be a very worthwhile pilgrimage.

It is always a struggle to pen everything down intelligently despite having the understanding and the information in one's head. The context of Indians in India (III) vs. Indians as Non Resident Indians (NRI) is vastly different and psychologically immensely more complex due to coping with myriad ethnic, religious, cultural, linguistic, political, and geographical diversity and challenges. Living in alien countries, even if by choice, challenges one's resilience, threatens one's self confidence, confronts one's values, disrupts familiar routine, and imposes unfamiliar stresses.

In essence, living in unfamiliar cultures forces one to learn new cues, routines, responses, etiquettes – and demands constant decision making. Imagine having to cope with all that and more without the familiar social-cultural-religious cues or support systems. The support systems are absent, institutions from school to community services are different and the work place demands exceptional proving of oneself. Even the climate becomes a source of stress.

Familiar entertainments do not exist and the formalities of time, place and person become necessary. Guests and friends cannot drop in any time and scheduling becomes a Herculean task due to too many pulls and pushes and the desire to follow the proper etiquette of the place you are in. Lunch no longer means having your paratha and pickle on your desk since – at least in the western countries – it's customary to step away from your work place in order to socialize, bond, network, etc. The need to hyper-focus on the task becomes secondary to being with peers, relaxing and renegotiating alliances.

In addition to the stresses and distresses of Indians living in different countries, they have additional factors that complicate a clinicians' understanding. These complications relate to the myriad variety of sub religions/sects, sub castes, origins from different provinces, language differences as well as physical characteristics. Just being Indian does not mean that cognitive, emotional and behavioral cultures are the same and therefore easy to grasp. The Indian Diaspora is probably the most diverse in the world

My leading and coordinating the Vanaprastha Corps, a voluntary, interdisciplinary psychological-addiction-marriage-family treatment program for the Indian Diaspora, has allowed me to interact with the wide and diverse communities both clinically and socially. Usually these projects took the form of Mental Health-Medical-Addiction treatment camps which also included teaching, training, and consulting in various countries of the Indian Diaspora.

It has always been my passionate desire to experience the essence of India, whether traveling within India from Kashmir to Kanyakumari, from Andaman to Ajmer, or visiting all the nations where the Indian Diaspora has settled. These journeys have taken me to crisscrossing the Silk Route, Alexander the Great's campaign route, retracing Mahatma Gandhi's footsteps, visiting Tinganes (the smallest capital in the world), taking a trip through villages where ancient Aramaic is still spoken, traveling to the Muslim shrines from Syria to Pakistan, exploring Jesus' life from Jerusalem, Bethlehem to Egypt, and climbing the mountaintops of Kailash to almost 20,000 feet in Tibet. I have crisscrossed the equator at least 3 times and have traveled the ends of the earth from Cape Horn to the Cape of Good Hope.

This book is dedicated to the Indian Diaspora and the mental health consumers and providers – now or in the making. Modern Mental health services for the Indian Diaspora is a recent development and it will be a slow process before the community learns to fully utilize them. Stigma and lack of familiarity with the psychologist/ psychiatrists' roles are major obstacles. Additionally, major challenges exist because the overall number of Indian mental health providers are few and far between and lacking in availability where the need is. Indian mental health practitioners have yet to take it upon themselves to educate the community at large. They are in the initial phase of establishing themselves as mental health entrepreneurs. Culturally, Indians prefer to become physicians, engineers, and teachers but not mental health professionals. Indian ethnic newspapers publish more articles on crime, food recipes, fashion and Bollywood than on mental health.

Mainstream media continues to report all Diasporic illegal acts as criminal instead of pointing out that many of them are the simply result of manic-depression, addictions, schizophrenia, and psychopathic or other personality disorders. As a result, dually diagnosable Indians end up in the prison system without any advocacy or support system.

In essence, the Indian Diaspora at large has yet to recognize the importance of good mental health as a prerequisite for marital, familial, intergenerational, and individual empowerment and well-being, whether related to work or to physical health. Spirituality begins where good mental health ends, and happiness is experienced only when one is free from physical and mental distress.

It is my intention that this book will make a difference in the lives of those who are struggling. Though the focus is on the Indian Diaspora, I am aware that many of the challenges discussed are ones we can all relate to, no matter what our culture or place of origin. At one time or another, we have all experienced being a "stranger in a strange land." The challenges are many and complicated, but there are more and more solutions, options and resources to help. Balance and transformation are possible. We can honor where we are from and enjoy life where we are.

Greesh C. Sharma, Ph.D., DMSP.
February 16, 2015

Acknowledgments

My lifelong determination was to someday become a respected psychologist, but I was uncertain whether it would happen, because I grew up in a small town where nothing much happened. But the path unfolded for me – many people helped me along the way.

Clinical psychology would not have been my passion without the inspiration of my deceased cousin, Yogendra Shanker Sharma. I would not have aspired to become a serious student of psychology if not for the nurturing of Professor J.G. Tripathi, and I would never have assimilated the trait to accept challenges without the goading of Professor Jai J. Tiwari, both in the psychology Department at Varshney College, Aligarh, UP. I was not alone in my class of peers subjected to their inspirations, but I was definitely the only one who excelled beyond their dreams.

I would be remiss if I didn't genuinely acknowledge the contribution of my biological family, psychologically significant others, tons of colleagues and friends, and over 30,000 patients. The contribution of patients in therapists' success is priceless as it pays twice: first monetarily and, second, through emotional growth. The contribution of my wife, Olga (Urmila) Sharma has been extremely crucial and I would not have realized my potential without her support, loving confrontations, daily teasing, and inspiration with deadlines to finish the book. I sought escape in traveling and playing chef but she brought me back to reality. This completed book is an example of her relentless rigorousness and making things happen. I am glad she was on my side. My daughter Bharati Sharma assisted me with proof reading of the book despite raising Deven, who was born on July 7, 2014.

Kelly Deeny's careful review of the content saved ample time. Dr. Vivianne Silverstein's feedback and encouragement proved very therapeutic during moments of self-doubt and made the book become reality. Last but not the least, Kumar Tadepalli's expertise, wisdom, patience and skills facilitated the entire process to complete this book.

I hope the book will be received for what it is – a reinforcement of the importance of mental health and acceptance of the variety of services available by rising above the stigma and the denials. However, the handbook is not a substitute to reaching out for help and exploring treatment options.

Introduction

This handbook is intended to be an easy guide for the Indian mental health consumer, regardless of their country of residence and political circumstances. This huge mass of one-billion-plus humanity shares a unique composition regardless of caste, regional, linguistic, provincial, religious and sub-cultural differences. Indians are known to be the most diverse people in the world. Among three major civilizations, China, Egypt, and India, it is the latter that has comparatively retained more of their uncontaminated originality. China buckled under the communist Cultural Revolution and Egypt lost its originality under the monopoly of Islam. Persian civilization had its apex but now it's insignificant due to its very small population. This is the century of the West; a dominant civilization setting the baseline and the ideals for the world. Globalization is the new world order and its negative side effects have yet to be determined.

> *"Present-day India is not a new civilization on an ancient soil, like Iran or Egypt. The living stream of Indian consciousness in the twentieth century is continuity, the same stream which has been steadily flowing for millennia. The Pyramids speak of the glory of an Egypt that is gone; the Mohenjo Daro is not a relic but an organism in the living culture of India."*
>
> *- Srimati Sophia Wadia: The Path of Satyagraha*

India remains a complex gestalt that comprises a deeply ingrained commonality of personality traits, uniformity of core character, predictable behavioral patterns, and essential fundamental values. In my travels I have often seen, as well as heard, that *you can take Indians out of India but not the India out of Indians*. Even when transplanted abroad, regardless of how long ago, their personal and interpersonal dynamics dominate their daily routines and ideals. Yes, they prefer to be invisible but never a social pariah, nor do they wish to interfere with other's way of life.

India too has had severe blows to its psyche, social order, and national character because of a past that includes 1100 years of foreign rule. Indian history is entrenched with trauma of Holocaust proportions. The genocide and the premeditated destruction of the Hindu libraries, universities, places of religious worship, burning of cities and towns was carried out by the Tatars, Persians, Uzbeks, Mongols, Afghans,

Portuguese, and British. The Hindu genocide continues unabated in Kashmir, Bangladesh, and Pakistan. They were exiled from Uganda and Afghanistan in recent times. In Fiji, the democratically elected government headed by an Indian was taken hostage by the army. Jews got the recognition of their holocaust but Hindus, Armenians, Tamilians in Sri Lanka and Cambodians still wait to be recognized and considered an endangered species.

Islamic conquest of India was the longest, bloodiest and most devastating threat to Hindu life, liberty, marriage, family, religious practices, culture, ideals and spirituality. Historians like Will Durant and Koenraad Elst have made such comments. Encyclopedia Britannica makes mention of the Mughal emperor, Akbar, ordering the massacre of 30000 captured Rajput Hindus on February 24, 1568, and that in December 1398, Taimurlane executed at least 50000 Hindus just before heading to Delhi. These are not exceptions and, for a curious reader, there is plenty of evidence that recognizes that the present Hindu national character has its origin in the Hindu holocaust i.e. Post-traumatic Stress Disorder. The trauma did not stop after the decline of Islamic rule, since the British Raj had continued the tradition of not only physically killing Indians, but even more so psychologically by the undermining of their marriage, family, personality, culture, religion and, in essence, the core of Indian identity.

The references to genocide, holocaust, and traumas are necessary in order to understand the historical roots of Indians' post-traumatic stress disorder. The psychology of victims and traumatized people is often very different from the ones who rule, perpetrate cruelty and snatch away the dignity of others. Indian mental health and personality alterations due to trauma are inseparable. People living in danger and with the anticipation of being raped, kidnapped, deprived of safety and security, or forcefully converted exhibit a pattern of confusion as to their identity, and experience more than usual anxiety, worries and vulnerability to depression.

The Indians' fear and anticipation of the past recurring paralyzes them and shutting down or becoming invisible becomes their best defense. Thoughts of anger, confrontation and challenging others evokes an overwhelming sense of danger and the possibility of being killed. Their ability to trust their own senses/faculties becomes compromised and they seek authentication and validation from others. They operate to appease authority and yet lose all sense of trust in the social and legal institutions. In essence, avoidance, apathy and invisibility becomes their modus operandi. Safety at any cost results in them identifying themselves as not really belonging to any religion, community or cause. This is the context which summarizes the Indian Diaspora and its mental health parameters.

Added complications include poor job opportunities, poverty, political threats, criminals seeing them as soft targets and, recently, the rising rate of alcoholism, suicide and breakdown of the traditional marriage and family.

The Indian word for crisis is *Aapati*, meaning holocaust, catastrophe, doom, gloom, danger, and utter helplessness; beyond the ability to defend. It is worth noting that only those people suffering from acute and chronic post-traumatic stress disorder (PTSD) tend to perceive and overreact to a crisis in such terms.

Historically, the British sent their unmanageable psychopaths to administer the colonies including India. Modern day invaders, marauders and psychopaths came to India in the guise of businessman, proselytizers and terrorists, exacerbating the after effects of PTSD and chipping away at the core values and, in essence, Indian national identity. In my observation, Hindus in particular, among the entire global Indian Diaspora, show the most pervasive traumatization and need to be invisible.

> *"Where the clear stream of reason has not lost its way*
> *into the dreary desert sand of dead habit.*
> *Where the mind is led forward by thee*
> *into ever widening thought and action.*
> *In to that heaven of freedom, my father,*
> *LET MY COUNTRY AWAKE!"*
>
> *- Rabindranath Tagore: Gitanjali*

However, it's not all gloom and doom. In spite of the external influences, Indians have spread all over the world and have resiliently managed the external context via their ingenuity and cultural continuity. Although their political and economic status varies greatly from country to country, the overall image of the diaspora is one that is positive and often emulated and envied. For one hundred fifty years, Indians have made significant contributions to their respective lands of adoption. Without exception, they tend to be a model minority, never victimizing other minorities, resorting to violence, or putting down people of other faiths. They live unpretentiously with regard to their wealth, education, or accomplishments. It is a group that in general does not create waves and prefers to accomplish very quietly and discreetly, deflecting all attention and remaining focused on the nitty-gritty of life.

Beneath the surface, despite this group's immense accomplishments, is an underlying collective inferiority complex syndrome under the façade of delusional self-importance. Indian history has left deep emotional scars on the psyche of the Indian diaspora. These scars reveal themselves in symptoms such as self-denigration, self-doubt, apathy, passivity, avoidance, denial, minimization of challenges and distancing from threats. Interestingly, Indians compensatory narcissistic sense of excessive self- importance is merely a veneer to cover up collective insecurity. Indians seek immunity in money, education and professional successes at the cost of good public relations and counteracting negative stereotypes.

"The key of India is in London."
Benjamin Disraeli: Speech, House of Lords, March 5, 1881

On an individual level, this sense of insecurity manifests itself in the form of apathy, passivity, minimal involvement, non-committal behavior and avoidance of seeing the "bigger psycho-socio-political picture". Such naiveté leaves the diaspora members vulnerable to aggressive locals, other minorities or competing social groups.

In Kenya, for example, natives saw Indians as traitors because they never invested in land and held their funds in the UK which was contrary to the Kenyans' culture values. Elsewhere in Africa, Indians related to the indigenous population only as laborer, worker and not at a household level.

On a national level, this insecurity reveals itself in how India relates to the rest of the world, which is often through the prism of seeking validation, acceptance from foreigners, Caucasian celebrities and Eurocentric authorities. Avoidance of confrontation is the most stress inducing and self-defeating Indian pattern. Nothing in India or about Indians is good enough unless the former colonial bosses (Europeans) or their American cousins say "it is good enough." The Indians' defensive mechanisms of feeling secure in mastering the art of monetary, academic, and professional excellence is creating a negative stereotype and a counterproductive interracial reputation. A lack of awareness of this dynamic has potential dangers for Indians as shown by the abrupt expulsion of Indians from Uganda in 1972.

The modern India's technical competence and military buildup is indeed impressive, but has done little to ease the struggles of either the Indian masses or that of its displaced, depressed & traumatized countrymen abroad. The Indian diaspora remains vulnerable as backlash from indigenous populations and other racial minorities loom larger than ever. For instance, the Indian Prime Minister in Fiji, despite being democratically elected, was thrown out and arrested by black Fijians. The 2009 arrest of the elected Prime Minister Mahendra Chaudhry, because he was Indian, the murder of hundreds of Indians in Malaysia during riots and ethnic violence, and the ethnic cleansing of Hindus in Pakistan, Bangladesh and Uganda, never even brought a word of condemnation from world leaders or the past Prime Ministers of India or by the Indian Muslims.

This paradox of apathy and detachment and simultaneously choosing to be passive by failing to see and anticipate others' reactions, and stoicism, fears and seeking invisibility are typical indicators of PTSD. Simultaneously, this cautious and evasive coping mechanism is also indicative of a colonial mindset, i.e. experiencing a pervasive sense of being rendered helpless almost to the extent of regressing to an infantile level. All personal power is relinquished to others, expecting magical relief and safety without exercising any sense of personal control or negotiating from strength. There are many lessons to be learned in juggling interracial relationships and projecting a positive image. Mental health is an important component of managing this complex set of dynamics, i.e. preventing further traumas and stressful interactions.

Magic via total complacency never happens. Bureaucrats and politicians do their thing, scientists sit in their fancy labs, and professors take comfort in their ivory towers, while the Indian Diaspora feels increasingly vulnerable and exhausted. A new generation of social scientists who are secure in their ethnic, racial, religious and national identity are needed to address the emotional, social and political challenges facing the Indian Diaspora. The collaboration and leadership needs to offer congruent solutions. The priority has to be the well-being of the marriage, family, intergenerational relationships *before* financial excellence.

Satya Prasad summarized the essence of this book as follows:

"This thoroughly researched and well-written book deals with the major mental health and other psychological problems facing the Indian diaspora in western countries. The cross-cultural conflicts lead to alcoholism, depression, mental illness, disruption of family life and other social problems. The author, a practicing psychologist, enunciates those problems and then offers solutions with practical examples. The book is useful both for professionals and general public. The exhaustive bibliography and comparison between the eastern and western concepts of the disease add to the value of the book. The contents of the book aptly justify its title, **Mental Health Survival Guide.**"

- Satya Prasad, M.P.A.,Ph.D.,
Ex-Research Fellow, UGC, India,
Retd. Sr. Research Associate. NJHMFA, New Jersey, USA

One admonition for the reader: when the term "Indian" is mentioned in the book, it is referring to more than 85% of the population of the Indian Diaspora who are Hindus. Of course, Indian Diaspora is known to be the most diverse in the world as it includes myriad variety of ethnicities, religions, and linguistic differences. It is India's uniqueness that diverse identities such as Muslims with their Arab-centric, Christians with Eurocentric, Parsis Zoroastrian-centric, and Jews with their Judeo-centric orientation have converged into a gestalt, giving rise to the Indian Diaspora of today.

It has been said that you can take an Indian out of India but not India out of an Indian. Hopefully, the book will prove to be a useful tool for the Diaspora. The information contained within is intended as mental health first-aid, easy steps to seeking professional help, and pointers to negotiating cost-effective and appropriate treatments. Every stress does not require a face-to-face consultation with a professional. The book can be utilized for self-help as well as offering counseling to others.

The sun never sets on the Indian Diaspora. Every seventh person on earth is an Indian. The Indian population emigration did not begin with the British. It is as old as time itself. The Indian Diaspora is spread out across 128 countries. There are an estimated 30,000,000 people of Indian origin living outside of India. According to the United Nations, the Indian Diaspora is the second largest after China in the world. Indian Diaspora means people of Indian origin (PIO) who may or may not be citizens of India at present. Another term used to identify Indian diaspora is Non-Resident Indian (NRI).Until 1948, current residents of Bangladesh and Pakistan were also referred to as Indians.

Indians have been traveling since ancient times. One can see the Indian religious artifacts in the museums of Latin America, particularly in Peru. Some scholars refer to three major waves of Indian migration. The Silk route probably resulted because of Indians settling for business reasons in Cambodia, Laos, Malaysia, Thailand, Burma, Afghanistan, Nepal and Indonesia. Many of these countries are often mentioned in the Hindu scriptures as though they are a part of an extended ancient India. Through the influence of Vedic culture, Hindu architecture as well as through the dissemination of Buddhism, Indian influence appears to have been pervasive. According to the Institute of American Religion census, there are an estimated 600,000 practicing Hindus and about 600 Mandirs in the USA. Similarly in most countries where Indians have settled, they have maintained their temples and other religious-cultural institutions.

During the British Raj of India, the need for cheap labor resulted in discontinuing slavery and, instead, calling it indentured labor. These laborers were instrumental in working the plantations throughout Africa, countries in the Indian Ocean, and the Caribbean. These plantations basically produced sugar, rubber and other farm products for European import. Often these indentured laborers were kept in poor conditions and were frequently never paid the contract return 4d fair. As a result, the majority ended up settling in the countries where were working. Proselytization and other legal maneuvers were utilized by the British government to dilute Indian culture. For example in Trinidad, individuals with Christian names were given priority. Cremation was also banned, affecting the Hindu way of life.

Post-Colonial migration, however, has been basically non-predatory except in the Gulf States. The treatment of Indian immigrants, like other Diasporas, depends upon the core culture and the value system of the host country. For example, Indians have flourished and contributed a great deal to the economies of the host countries which practice democracy, transparency and multiculturalism. Canada, USA, UK, Australia and New Zealand have been model host countries.

However, the same is not true for Indians working in Middle East/Arab countries. Africa has been a different story since new Indians have gone in recent days as teachers and professors. Post-colonial emigrants largely have been skilled and professionals. However, in the Gulf

States, many have gone as domestic help, laborers, farm servants along with engineers and other professionals in education and the oil industry. It depends on the educational level of the immigrant and the response of the host country.

The India of today is different as it is recognizing the human resource power of the Persons of Indian Origin. She is waking up to the realization that the Indian diaspora in the west has the "know how" and wealth. Their successes, specialties and character transformation offers India the potential for volunteers, readymade mentors, and relatively corruption free leaders. India's exports to meet the need of the Diaspora communities adds to India's foreign exchange reserve. But more so, Indians as informal ambassadors of India have the influence and the capital to lobby on India's behalf. It is a mutually beneficial dependence between the Indian Diaspora and India. A mutually healthier trust, appreciation and fast track development of Non-Resident Indians (NRI) related services, institutions and opportunities will go a long way toward India Shining.

It's the NRI and the People of Indian Origin (PIO) who are responsible for the turmericazation (Indian influence on other cultures) of many countries in the world. It's India's turn to be an empowered mother and homeland for its Diaspora to realize her ambitions to become an incredible India and a super power. The Chinese Diaspora contributes more foreign exchange to China than The Indian Diaspora contributes to India. The Chinese Diaspora has also been smarter than Indians in making Little Chinas – that look like an extension of their homeland – all over the world and, in the process, becoming tourist attractions. This creates jobs and economic opportunities. It's one of the reasons that Chinese food has become mainstream while Indian food is just emerging as worth mentioning in comedy shows and literary circles.

Chinese success in making Little Chinas so appealing to tourists and the mainstream population is rooted in their asserting their culture through architecture (pagodas, dragons, floral designs, etc.), providing essentials (groceries, stores, restaurants, etc.), and having their places of worships as well as community centers concentrated in a specific pocket of the city. Indians shy away due to their tendency to stay invisible and fear of negative reactions from non-Indians. As a consequence, "Indianity" always is the last to become mainstream.

As can be seen from this brief survey, emigrants from India are a heterogeneous lot. Migrant circumstances create a variety of factors that include numbers of migrants, periods of migration, treatment by their host countries, their regional and linguistic backgrounds, and the orientation of the Diasporic Indians to their native land. As William Safran notes (2005), it is a general characteristic of diasporics that "they continue to relate, personally or vicariously, to their homeland in one way or another, and their ethno-communal consciousness and solidarity are importantly defined by the existence of such a relationship." In Hindu Manners, Customs and Ceremonies, by Abbe J.A. Dubois, Henry K. Beauchamp wrote, "Even when [Indians] migrate or travel from one province to another, natives of India never throw off what I may call the characteristics of their native soil. In the midst of their new surroundings they invariably preserve their own language and customs." (Page 11'Third Ed. Oxford at the Clarendon Press, 1928)

The Indian Diaspora loves to take pride in boasting about how many corporations have Indian brains and manpower behind them, and that average Indian's income is much higher than that of an American, etc. Neither the Indian ethnic press nor the Diaspora in general ever dares to allow mention of the imperfections, vulnerabilities and epidemics of social pathologies. There is a flip side to all the political, financial and academic successes of the Indian diaspora.

Underneath the veneer of modal minority, above average income in western countries, suburban prosperous living, winning the spelling bees and having one or more Governors, Ms. World, and a few judges, attorney generals and even a handful of appointments to the White House, the Indian Diaspora is showing signs of fatigue. This weariness is not limited only to the USA and western countries, but pervades the Indian diaspora in the Caribbean and Indian Ocean countries as well. Indian ethnic newspapers often devote a page or more to the crimes committed by Indians. Recently, Dateline NBC's, *To Catch a Predator*, showed Indians being caught in soliciting sex with minors. There is no reason to fantasize that the Indian Diaspora will continue to remain a modal minority and not be in the news for sniper shootings, sexual perversions, stealing credit cards and others' identity, psychotic episodes in public and bizarre acting out while in manic phase of the bipolar episode.

On the other hand, the Diaspora cousins who severed the umbilical cord with Mother India about 150 or so years ago, are beyond fatigued as they are experiencing a major collapse of their financial network, cultural values, and traditions as well as ethnic, familial and marital disintegration. Fiji has Indian prostitutes/sex workers. Suriname has polygamy. Trinidad has a major alcohol epidemic. Guyanese Indians are fearful of leaving their house due to being targeted by criminals and drug addicts.

Tamilians in Sri Lanka are living like refugees. Even in India, Punjab is under the grip of pervasive drug addiction and many other provinces are in ruins with regard to law and order. Suicides in India are an epidemic. India Abroad, in its issue of July 4, 2014, reported that Jayanti Naik, only 14 years old, committed suicide because her parents could not afford to pay for a pencil and a notebook. More than 6000 Indians are languishing in foreign jails with 1400 in Saudi Arabia for visa related crimes to robbery. India Tribune reported on May 10, 2013 that Indians are among the top three nationalities that steal items from hotel rooms abroad, followed by Mexicans and Columbians. However, the favorite crime committed by Indians tends to be financial fraud.

This rapid rise in social pathologies is not limited to the Indian Diaspora. But here our focus is on Indian Diaspora since it's closely tied to mental health and also to the damaging public image. For example, a person addicted to alcohol or drugs is liable to commit crimes to support the habit or because of impaired judgment. Persons with limited intelligence can behave socially inappropriately or display childlike behavior. A person suffering from Bipolar disorder and having a manic episode can engage in inappropriate sexual behaviors with minors, steal someone's money, drive over the speed limit or walk naked in the middle of the highway.

The rise in Indian Diaspora social pathology and decline in moral fabric is not an inherent character defect but a result of complex socio-geo-econo-political context in which they have lived so far. Additionally, the breakdown of the marriage, family and communities, as in other Diasporas, is also a major contributory factor. Statistics are not available as to the mental problems or crimes of and by Indians since no one has the resources, or has even come to realize the relevance of it. Even Indian Ph.D. students do not make it a priority to research issues pertaining to the Diaspora. Often non-Indians tend to write about issues pertaining to India, Indian Diaspora, Indian marriage and culture but rarely insiders. Indians have always preferred to see themselves defined by others. However, it is apparent that Indian Diaspora is on the decline since its keepers have gone in hibernation. It is visible to the naked eye that poverty, unemployment, alcoholism, marital and family breakdown, lack of resources and services in the Indian Diaspora are furthermore compounded due to the hostilities, prejudices and discrimination by the indigenous or non-Indian communities.

Despite the common perception in the developed world of overseas Indians as a prosperous, professional breed, it is important to understand that many of the thirty million Indians living outside of India are subject to discrimination, terrorism, murder and other forms of violence, forced conversions, ethnic cleansing, temple destruction, socio-political alienation and disenfranchisement. In some countries, fundamentalists from other religions advance a discriminatory and non-inclusive agenda and promote hatred of religious and ethnic minorities in league with military, politicians and other government officials. In smaller island countries the Diaspora is vulnerable to backlash from the indigenous population as they see Indians as a soft target i.e. they never retaliate or confront. Abbe J.A. Dubois, A French missionary described Hindus as, "The mental faculties of the Hindus appear to be as feeble as their physique." (Page 321)

Individual mental health is a good starting point. Of course, the sole focus on mental health will not solve all the social pathologies of the Diaspora but it is the most cost effective medium to promote the individual, marital and family functioning. A proactive approach will empower the Diaspora with improved leadership, a sense of purpose and direction and improved networking to invite Indian professionals. The need for mental health programs, medical and other support services is dire. Any delayed action will have catastrophic implications. The denial phase is over.

It is time to bring everything to light. Disowning vulnerabilities, stresses, threats, and illnesses is if no use. Bravery and courage are in facing and not hiding, and they are the first steps towards taking charge.

It's a reality that most of the developing Third World countries either do not recognize mental health as a national priority or are in the initial stages of econo-political development. Governments cannot be relied upon to offer programs or resources. Politicians' priorities and resources are directed by ulterior motives of ensuring hold on power and not necessarily by the psycho-somato-socio-spiritual urgencies of the masses.

Once I visited Zambia, which has no mental health system in existence. While driving with an Indian family towards Victoria Falls (Zimbabwe), we saw a stranded Indian family on the roadside. My host stopped, in spite of the major inconvenience and extended the necessary help. He explained to me "we look after our own". I have visited most countries that are home to the Indian Diaspora and in almost all developing countries from the African continent to the Caribbean, mental health services are practically non-existent or minimally available or non-accessible. The mentally ill are still treated either as possessed by evil spirits, misunderstood as criminals, or simply ignored. Apathy frees one from taking any personal responsibility.

In this regard, developed countries like the USA, Canada, Australia, New Zealand and the UK, etc. have added experience, resources and an established system to help or take care of the emotionally needy. They offer a ready-made blue print and short cuts to duplicating mental health services, but of course money, professionals and volunteers have to be provided by the Diaspora in the specific countries.

Such a coordination of needs, contact between users and providers on both sides will require initiative. The best place to start is by identifying a list of needs. The Internet has made the world very small. Indian Diaspora needs an Indian Hot Line (crisis intervention) for prevention, treatment and referral. Even the Indian government is now listening, as well as the Indian members of all the professional organizations, whether medicine, psychology, social work or law.

I am optimistic that Indian international corporations may be open to extend their resources, provided the host community has the leadership to initiate and coordinate such need-based requests. Of course the resource provider has to be given a guarantee that the request is genuine i.e. for the collective good. The information and exchange process is only as far as using the Internet or writing a letter. Indian embassies and consulates also can be a productive liaison in coordinating preventive mental health workshops, conferences and community education events.

Surveys conducted by various Indian diaspora advocacy groups indicate that human right violations like the chronic PTSD caused by ancient invaders, continue to do irreparable psychological damage to the minorities – ranging from mental breakdown to relinquishing their religious faith, traditions and culture. They feel coerced into giving up their identity in order to protect their women, children and elders. Historical background is relevant whether establishing diagnosis of patient or deciphering one's psychological identity. Geo-political context of a person also becomes important in order to understand their problem solving approach and unique reactions to threats.

Geo-political realities facing Indian Diaspora differ from country to country. It appears that Indians are thriving more in the West than in island countries, with the exception of Mauritius. The following are country-specific first impressions regarding the Indian Diaspora and their mental health options.

People's Republic of Bangladesh

Bangladesh is the saddest story of the Indian Diaspora. The Hindu population has been decimated and the entire community terrorized. There is no law and order ensuring a minority's safety. There is an international silence surrounding the human rights violations by Bangladesh. Religious tensions are high and most Hindus wish to settle in India. Wendy Schuljan wrote in a letter to the editor of Hinduism Today, June 2000, "The genocide of three million people, mostly Hindus, makes me feel so sad."

I visited Bangladesh during the third week of February 2000. During my encounter with numerous Hindu families, I learned that they felt absolutely vulnerable, unsafe, depressed, traumatized, and desperate. Their collective sense of post-traumatic stress disorder is rooted in reality, as the absence of law and order, and victimization by fundamentalists and criminals have made many feel unable to continue living in that country. They feel they cannot protect their women and children or practice Hinduism due to Islamists' interference. At the same time they feel abandoned by India and the Hindu Diaspora at large. Mental health services are minimal, not accessible and social stigma keeps them from seeking help.

Republic of the Fiji Islands

I visited Fiji in October of 1996. During my lecture tour there, I was fortunate to have personal and trusting interactions with native blacks but also many Indians. The dynamics were fascinating. There was no mutual trust or respect. Natives saw Indians as greedy, money-minded, and arrogant while Indians saw blacks as unreliable, untrustworthy, and unaccountable. I learned that most Indians own businesses and when they have black employees, they expect them to open the business on time, be there, and handle their personal life before or after work. However, due to the natives' tribal roots, they have little awareness of time or punctuality. Indigenous people live informal lives based on their moods, events and feelings. For example, if there is a death in the tribal village, they may not show up to work for months.

I have observed this dilemma in most countries where Indians have settled and natives have a different culture and value system or are in significant numbers. Indians do not have a comfort zone in Fiji due to political and native's negative stereotyping of Indians. A monk, Vyasa Prasad wrote in 2000, "Right now a pall of gloom hangs over the Fiji Indian community – there is pain and distress." Mental health services are minimal. They are treated in a general hospital by a regular physician. There are a handful of mental health academicians of New Zealand origin.

Indian State of Jammu and Kashmir

I visited Srinagar in 2004. I have never seen any place on Earth so heavily militarized. Most Hindus have been pushed out and even the local Muslim population is mortified by Islamists. During one of my conversations, a local Muslim teacher in a soft whisper, due to fear, shared with me that, in his view, Muslims have been extremely unfair to Kashmiri Pundits. If Islamization of Kashmir is a sample as to what happens to minorities, then it is a nightmare and definite trigger of mental health calamity for other religious groups. I have spoken to a few Kashmir refugees in the USA who are clearly demonstrating symptoms of overwhelming sense of abandonment, helplessness, depression and post trauma.

Kingdom of Bhutan

I visited Bhutan during the second week of February, 2005. On the surface, the country was peaceful and welcoming. I was surprised to later learn that Hindus have been exiled and discriminated against in large numbers. I have met many Hindu Bhutanese refugees in the USA. On the whole, they seem a happy people, but are traumatized by being uprooted and rendered homeless & helpless. The USA has given them sanctuary but their struggle surrounding poverty, language difficulties and cultural shock continues to overwhelm them. In Bhutan, there were no mental health services available, except those that were informally carried out by Buddhist monks.

Malaysia

I was there in 1997 and again in 2003. My contacts were limited so I have no authentic voice to speak about the mindset of Malaysian Indians. However, news clippings have revealed major distrust and mutual blaming between the Indian Diaspora and Malaysian government which is ethnically Muslim. The Government blames Indians for committing more serious crimes than any other group.

Indians blame the government for being racist and treating them as second class human beings. Malaysia is an ethnic boiling point. Hundreds of Indians were killed during ethnic riots in 1969 and it is anticipated that it will repeat.

However, if a Hindu is either in love with or married to a Muslim woman, he loses all rights and has to follow Sharia law from marriage to burial. The implication is that a Hindu cannot truly practice his or her own religion and cultural values. Like most other Muslim countries, mental health is not adequately developed nor there is any hope in the near future that such help will be available. Indians are trapped in a very difficult paradox since they see themselves as Malaysians but without the sense of protection, safety or justice. It's a perfect context for emotional illnesses like depression, domestic violence, nervous breakdown, suicide or acting out violently.

Islamic Republic of Pakistan

I visited numerous cities in Punjab and Sindh and most of the historical and religious sites in Pakistan during 2005. I was fortunate to have close encounters with Pakistani Hindus as well as Muslims. Pakistanis were kind and very hospitable. However, they were subdued in their admiration of Indian democracy and success, but openly envious. They were all critical of crime, and lack of law and order in Pakistan. On the surface no chaos was visible but in discussions Muslims as well as Hindus admitted to being very fearful

Hindus in Pakistan live under barbaric conditions, having no rights, respect, acceptance, safety, or protection under the law. They are forcefully evicted from their farm lands and houses. Bonded labor is still pervasive even though outlawed in 1992 and Hindus are even bought and sold. Sind's agriculture depends upon bonded labor, mostly tribals and Hindus of the untouchable caste called Haris. Feudal landlords still rule as they have always done in certain areas and provinces and consider labor as their property.

The Guardian on March 18, 1996 wrote, "So much so…landlord Ibrahim Mangrio did not worry about witnesses when he grabbed Meran Devi by the hair and dragged her into the field". She said, "He would rape me in front of my mother, he would rape me in front of the entire world." Kidnappings and forced marriages of minor girls is commonplace. If a girl is 9 years old, she may be kidnapped and married forcefully without the consent or presence of her parents. Pakistani Human Rights activists have verified these facts. The Hindu population has been reduced to negligible numbers due to forced conversions. Waqf manages all Hindu temples and Gurudwaras.

Ironically, many Pakistani Hindus have tried to immigrate to India but returned as they felt unwelcome and found no opportunities for work. It is amazing that Pakistan has the most significant Indian historical and civilization sites such as Harappa, Mohenjodaro, and Taxilla, but Indians are unable to visit or are denied visas. In spite of the funds being provided by UNESCO, these sites are deteriorating rapidly due to a lack of maintenance and outright neglect. As these sites symbolize the apex of Hindu civilization, it seems that Pakistanis would rather have them disappear.

It is not hard to imagine the mental health issues of the Indian Hindus in Pakistan. If that's not Hindu holocaust, then what? Typically living under oppression, perpetual fear, lacking any personal space safe and failure to protect their families, present day conditions of Hindus are a replica of Hindu life during Islamists' rule of India. Major depression, generalized anxiety disorder and post-traumatic stress disorder are common reactions to not being allowed to have an identity, to feel safe and result from living in perpetual helplessness and hopelessness.

Democratic Socialist Republic of Sri Lanka

I visited Sri Lanka in 2004 during the height of civil strife and tension between Tamilians and Sinhalese. As a tourist, I did not notice or have the opportunity to learn much from personal encounters. However, the news reports detailed violence and pervasive mutual distrust between Tamilians and Sinhalese. My visit to Tamilian Tiger territories was tense and the signs and scars of militarization and battles were all over. Ever since the Tamilian surrender, the reports of human rights violations and extreme victimization of the Tamilian population since May 2009 continues as per newspapers and some Human Right organizations. Once again, PTSD and major depression, and generalized anxiety are expected to be pervasive.

Sri Lanka does have an awareness of mental health issues and some services are available. However, these services are limited to only large cities and are underutilized due to ignorance, denials and the stigma of mental illness. Tamilians have even lesser access due to living in villages and remote areas.

Republic of Trinidad and Tobago

I visited Trinidad and Tobago in December of 2007. Trinidad is known to be a reputable vacation paradise. Hindus have been under pressure since the British to convert to Christianity, as cremation was banned and people with Christian names were given priority for jobs and other forms of advancements. Politics of conversion aside, Hindus have been experiencing a great deal of domestic violence, marital and family disintegration, suicides and alcoholism. Unlike in Mauritius and Fiji, the Indian Diaspora is showing signs of chronic fatigue and, as a result, is losing its grounding in culture and heritage.

Alcoholism, divorce, domestic violence, etc. are on the rise. No organized mental health services exist at a community level. There are many temples, but due to bhakti (devotion through ritualistic worship) orientation, none engage in offering crisis intervention, counseling or social services. Churches have done a reasonable job in offering pastoral counseling. Overall mental health utilization has not become part of the society and it is also not a national priority. Very few mental health services are available and there is also a dearth of alcohol and drug treatment programs. However, Alcoholic Anonymous meetings are available in larger cities.

Self-perceptions determine one's public image, and others' perceptions in turn determine self-perceptions. Apathy towards this psychological phenomenon can be potentially very costly in carrying out the business of living, raising family, working, succeeding, and feeling secure. One will not know how one is being perceived unless one is looking for it and is also willing to manage it.

A 35 year old, Caucasian American female from the upper middle class, once wrote to me in response to my question as to what she thinks of Indians. She said, "I have always been drawn intuitively to your culture. I thought Indians were highly spiritual beings, spending much time in meditation, prayer and the practice of yoga. I also thought most were vegetarians. I have always enjoyed listening to the way Indians speak the English language. I assume that family (extended and immediate) is far more important in the Indian culture than in ours". These are my personal views and now let me give you a glimpse of what I have heard many of my peers say: "Indians are cheap, as customers, dotheads challenging any price they see in the store, expecting us to lower it. They always shop together as families and never smile or attempt to converse with us Americans". She further stated that when she had agreed to see an Indian psychologist, "all

Indian men are sexist, misogynists and there is no way he will understand your perspective as a woman."

Public stereotyping of Indians, universally, can be summarized as follows (The order of listing is arbitrary and without any clinical significance): cheap, obsessed with finding bargains, negotiating even when shopping in a fixed price shop, maximizing return value of every penny, unscrupulous, socially never smiling or conveying warmth, lacking interest in others, self-preoccupied , narcissistic, hyper-focused on taking at the cost of sacrificing peer relationships or allowing the organic process to evolve, obsessed with results/bottom line, lacking basic courtesy, invasive and prying, apathetic as to how they are portraying negative image, having bad odor, unaware with regards to dressing inappropriately in public, disrespectful of the honor system, socially insecure, professionally rigid, and busy with self-importance.

It is often said that Indians go to any extent – from extreme invisibility to denying a religion or patriotic feelings for India. In this process of needing to be accepted, Indians tend to bad mouth everything. Their apologetic behavior is a veneer for defensiveness. Often Indian children born or raised here, feel embarrassed by their parents' economic preoccupations, social inadequacies and having a very narrow perspective on most things. They see them as obsessive, micromanagers and insecure. A list of Indian character defects probably will require a thousand pages but the essence is clear. The issue here is not that other ethnicities and nationalities are perfect, but simply that how others see Indians impacts the Indian Diaspora. Negative stereotypes are at a high risk.

Take the example of Jews. It was the negative stereotypes that resulted in the Holocaust. Indians, too, have experienced such traumas of lessor proportion in Uganda, Kenya, Fiji, Bangladesh, Pakistan, Sri Lanka and elsewhere. On the opposite side, the Japanese image is one of being honorable, trustworthy, proud, socially very considerate, fair and fun people. Germans, too, are seen as extremely punctual, responsible, honorable, trustworthy and having an excellent civic sense. Americans evoke a mixed image of being self-confident, sociable, friendly, highly pragmatic, easy going, individualistic, rushed, lacking European-like etiquettes and graces. In the hierarchy of stereotypes, my guess is Indians rank lower than Thais, Vietnamese, Cambodians, Sri Lankans, Singaporeans, Filipinos, and Koreans. It's not all negative, as Indians have positive sides to their image as well i.e. caring doctors, brilliant professors, astute lawyers, owners and operators of businesses, warm and caring at a personal level and loyal friends.

In reality, every ethnic, national and religious group has its own uniqueness and individuality, which manifests in their life style, perception of self, others and the world view. Additionally, cultural groups also display their character via certain preferences in terms of their academic, professional, entrepreneurial, social, and cultural ideals, choices and pursuits. This can be termed as their "national-mind" or "collective consciousness" which determines attitudes and directs the gestures and behavior of its people. These collective behaviors become associated and assigned by other ethnic groups to define people.

No national character is perfect. To decipher a national character is a herculean task. Character analysis as a pursuit has been given up by sociology and psychology for fear of political incorrectness. We all know what it is but we have agreed to keep silent. When we are relating to Japanese, Germans, Chinese, Pakistani or Americans, we know their modus operandi as to how they handle punctuality, sense of honor, civic duty, hygiene, etc. We all have stereotyped almost every nationality, ethnic and religious group. Indians evoke extremely ambivalent feelings in others. It has always been the case that Indians are admired for their positives and hated for their negatives.

No one seems to like being neutral as to the Indian character. In particular, those who see Indians through Eurocentric colored glasses tend to find nothing acceptable, tolerable or admirable about Indians. It is safe to state that Indian national character is a double edged sword. It evokes extreme reactions from others in spite of Indians' collective efforts to be invisible.

As stated and elaborated on earlier, modern day Indians' traumatic historical experiences have provided the "push" and determined a large part of their character and behavior. Hinduism is the oldest religion in the world and it, too, defines Indians and their scriptural ideals and cultural destination which acts as a "pull".

Individually or collectively, whenever you truly get to know someone, stereotypes get peeled away and you see the reality of the person behind the ideas about the person. To fully understand Indian character and begin to break free of the stereotypes, it is important to untangle as to where Indians are coming from and where they are going. Even of greater importance is to ask the question as to why they so very unique in their understanding of the universe, interdependence of all living things, belief in spirituality before materialism and, above all, boundless tolerance of everything that is different.

While India never lost sight of the necessity of the material and intellectual dimension of life, she laid a particular emphasis on the moral and spiritual aspect. Indians institutionalized tradition of Brahmacharya, Grahastha, vanaprastha and Sanyasa ashram to provide a structure to meet somato-psycho-socio-spiritual needs. Indians realize and perpetually worry that the nature of the nature is a perpetual dance between pull and push, good and evil, pain and pleasure, fear and courage, inside and outside, clinging and autonomy. Indian religious psychologies offered detachment by seeing life happenings as an illusion (Maya). In practical terms, life was organized to deal with reality, and to live responsibly through four stages i.e. Brahmacharya, Grahstha, vanaprastha and Sanyasa.

Spirituality in Hindu philosophies is described as an unconditional commitment to oneness with all creation. Hindu religion, on the other hand, prescribes the ideals and the procedures of dedicating one's life to the perfection of the soul or self-realization. Hindu pursuit of becoming free from it all (moksha) is rooted in seeing birth to death phases of life as pure punishment and suffering. One can see a Hindu's psychological dilemma of being born associated with suffering and being driven to the goal of merging into god so to be free from all suffering.

Hindus self-perception of being divine and uniting with divinity demands deliberate living via good karmas and avoiding all attachments. The Indian philosophical-psychology tradition, from the period of Vedas up to the modern time, presents an amazing record of reflection on man's nature, interpersonal dynamics, and human destiny. Spinoza has correctly said that "the intellectual love of God" is a summary of Hindu philosophy. Hindu philosophy basically addresses psycho-socio-health-spiritual aspects of human beings in the most relevant contexts ranging from personal growth, family and social functioning to global harmony and prosperity.

Indian civilization is essentially spiritual. It is not religious but is rooted in the highest ideals of secular humanity, i.e. we are all one and the same and divine in our origin and nature. In religious terms it is defined as dharma and not "religions." Dharma requires a continuous and sincere pursuit of the sacred over and above dogmas or any external central religious authority or control. There are no commandments but only personal responsibility. People of India have a strong sense of individuality and, at the same time, a sense of society at large, which enables them to think in terms of the common interests of groups and classes. Spread over a huge geographical area, `Indianity'–the essence of this polymorphous culture–is difficult to define. It acquires different postures and modes according to the tastes, attitudes, and mental sets of different groups and people united by an unspoken acceptance of certain constant social and cultural factors, such as the caste system, the belief in the cycle of successive lives, and sense of nationhood.

Every culture or society, even indigenous tribes, have ideals to which it they aspire. They do not have to be lofty and esoteric. The desired destination for Hindus is Nirvana, i.e. total freedom from any and all attachments, karmic vicious cycle, dependence on any object and, in essence, sustaining emotional equanimity. The following are rather overly simplified core conceptual pillars of Hindu character:

- Non-injury to any living thing or even to the plant as well as nature is the most indispensable aspect. From Vedic times to Buddha, Ashoka, and Mohandas Gandhi, all have been prophets of non-violence.
- Oneness with everything is the core belief of Hindus. This involves seeing self even in the smallest and most invisible creature and in friends and foes, each being an extension of one's own self.
- Relinquishing all desires, attachments, identities, possessions, and needing to control nothing is the Hindu psychology procedure to dealing with life. It is the Hindu way of managing the perpetual dance between Sympathetic and Parasympathetic nervous systems of a person. Mind is defined as a monkey; constantly jumping and moving. The modern clinical parallel is Attention Deficit Hyperactivity Disorder.
- Non-reactivity as opposed to reactivity is the prescribed cognitive-behavioral management tool for a Hindu. As a result, most of the Hindu practices such as meditation, yoga, fasting, silence from talking, etc. are all geared toward controlling and managing the sympathetic nervous system i.e. fight-flight trap. One should be neutral in pleasure or pain, defeat or conquest, praise or criticism, or loss versus gain and dominance of parasympathetic nervous system makes it feasible.
- Hindus subordinate actions to feelings, feelings to thought, thought to duty (dharma) and duty must be without any anticipations or expectations (subjectivity).
- Unlike other cultures, Hindus believe that from anger arises delusion, from delusion arises loss of memory, from loss of memory arises the loss of pure reasoning, and from loss of pure reasoning arises destruction. In other words, unlike in Western culture, negative feelings (anger, fear, desire, worrying, jealousy,

sadness) are not just managed externally but must be addressed at its source of origin, i.e. thought and desire.

- In Hindu psychology, the self is above intellect, "I", "mind", "five senses", "five motor organs," and the "five potentials". The Bhagavada Gita-based psycho-dynamics of emotional distress is defined by the following sequences:

- Abdominal-Anal-Genital Attachment -> Desire -> Anger -> Confusion > resulting in the Loss of Memory -> Destruction of Intelligence -> loss of ability of Discrimination. Therefore operating with a clear mindset of detachment guarantees good mental hygiene. Detached action is not synonymous with not caring but just the opposite i.e. total dispassionate focus and commitment to action.

- Ego pathology consists of ignorance which binds us to subjective behavior, narcissistic ways, prejudices, habits, conditioning, compulsions driven by likes and dislikes, and finally, in most cases, resulting in clinging, dependency, or addiction. Ego in the Eastern psychology is defined differently from the Freudian term as "executive functioning of the mind". In Hindu philosophies ego is defined as concept of self (I, Me, Mine) rooted in senses based in relating to the object (concrete reality). Often it's mere projection of our mind (Maya) and not of true self. Senses are under the control of the mind which is viewed as a monkey (impulsive and hyperactive) and object reality (external world) is defined as always transient and fluid. Therefore, approaching it as if it's solid and permanent merely triggers suffering i.e. emotional pathology.

A warning is indicated as to the practical aspect of Hinduism. In spite of its high ideals, unparalleled wisdom, fascinating insights into human nature and abundance of psychological procedures for good mental hygiene and treatment of mental illness, it fundamentally fails to deliver in terms of challenges on the ground. The significance gets lost in the loftiness of the high thinking. Buddhism and Sikhism emerged as simplified pragmatic Hinduism. They are easy to understand. It's actually not the Hindu psychologies that are hard to practice, but the practitioners who fail to integrate thought, feelings, talking and action. In other words, talking becomes a substitute for real cohesive action.

The roots of Indian spirituality were defined in the Vedic period, between 2000 and 500 BCE. During this period, the Vedas, the oldest scriptures of Hinduism, were composed. In terms of time, Hinduism precedes all Abrahamic faiths.

Deterioration of Indian art, culture and thought started with the decline of the Gupta Period (500 AD), which is known as one of the "Golden Ages of India." Most of the energy and imagination of Indians was used up avoiding cultural adulteration, to protect the purity of their identity. They accomplished this by imposing extreme taboos and restrictions on intermingling with alien invaders. This attitude was further reinforced by various rituals, caste consciousness, and untouchability. This negative development of discrimination introduced divisiveness with long term psychological, social, cognitive, and emotional consequences.

In medieval India, the intellectual life was embedded in the teachings of Hindu and Muslim mystic saints. Most of them denounced idolatry, the caste system, and untouchability. They also condemned polytheism and believed in one god. The seventeenth century marked the apex of India's medieval feudal culture. At the beginning of the 18th century the Mughal structure began to crumble. The British took full advantage of the weakness and of the follies of the Indian feudal rulers, Hindu and Muslim alike. Thus, another era of oppression started from 1757 onwards.

From the last decade of the medieval period to the beginning of modern times, Indian thought was in the grip of darkness. With no notable progress in the realm of thinking, political subjugation brought all-round demoralization to Indians. The English education system in India, as introduced by British rule, to a great extent influenced the minds of educated men. They became great admirers of everything Western and in the course of time came to develop an inferiority complex and an attitude of contempt towards the great religious and cultural traditions of their own country. This was the second time after the Indian holocaust, perpetrated by the Islamists, which the Indian mind was thrown into pervasive identity disintegration.

The Muslim invasions and conquests had initiated the ground work for the Indian scholars to experience poor self-esteem and trauma and lead to their seeking endorsement and legitimacy of their ideas in western literature and validation in the western world. The average Indian knew more about Shakespeare, William Wordsworth, Shelly and Keats than about Rabindranath Tagore, Premchand or any of the scholars from South India. It was the Indian's hobby to display their machismo by quoting western authorities. This "other orientation", "dependence proneness" and "safety in being a follower" of Indians was so exaggerated that their own reasoning ability and creativity were blunted and stifled until very recently. Historically, the intellectual autonomy, interpersonal effectiveness and productivity of Indian intellectuals became even more feeble minded as they co-opted first the Persian and later the Eurocentric/British way of looking at the self. Unfortunately, now it's Americanization and Globalization that is dictating life style, communication patterns and interpersonal relationships.

As a result of the British-India encounter, Indians developed a schizoid personality, best reflected in the famous characterization of Indians by Thomas Babington Macaulay, who in 1835 introduced English education to India: "Their skin is still brown, but their mind is colonial." It seems safe to predict that this composite character will continue to develop and that Indians will develop more of the excesses of modern, global culture, i.e. consumerism, loss of traditions, and the fragmentation of marriage and the nuclear family. It may be a sad journey for most of the Indian Diaspora since the countries they reside in are not equipped to deal with their particular mental health issues. Loss of Identity is choosing to be doomed into nothingness. Opting for cultural extinction is indicative of community shared mental illness bordering on Avoidant Personality Disorder. The opposite is holocaust when one is forced extinction

Indian Identity

From a distance, things appear rather pretty and idealistic. But the aerial view is never a substitute for the ground realties. As stated earlier, human behavior is a complex interaction of where one is coming from (past) and where one is going to (imagined or anticipated future). An individual who is unaware of the past journey and the destination is either brain damaged, psychotic, lost or may be a true yogi – free from all conditioning (samskaras). The memories are mere cumulative emotional associations and images as a result of inner and external encounters. Every encounter in life makes an impact; negative or positive. Perceptions and images, too, are a product of one's psychological journey. It all becomes glued together under the rubric of personality i.e. unique bundle of concepts, beliefs, thoughts, values and behavioral patterns.

Personality keeps one grounded from feeling anchorless. Individual personality can be "healthy" or troubled and dysfunctional. Mahatma Gandhi is an example of Healthy personality, while Emperor Aurengjeb and Hitler are examples of a morbid dysfunctional personality. Healthy personality in comparison to dysfunctional is defined in terms of being balanced, wholesome and full of empathy and compassion for others.

Human personality, character formation – even time tested belief systems, as well as concepts to process internal and external reality, evolve in the context of Geo-socio-econo-political–religious circumstances. Most people respond to the context passively. However, a handful few redefine and redesign the context. Gautama Buddha was a product of Vedic culture, aristocratic background, and royal lineage but chose to walk away from the prevailing context and altered it by offering a simpler, more direct, manageable, autonomous, and precise version of Hinduism. He bypassed the Vedas based, caste hierarchy, Brahmanic monopoly, and the controlled and rituals-based Sanatan (traditional) culture.

One's sense of identity is essential as it becomes a psychological framework to process perceptions about self, others and the world. In absence of this context, one merely exists as a generic human being and is vulnerable to incessant external pushes and pulls. Identity is not just a set of physical characteristics but layers of psychological aspects i.e. personal, familial, religious, social, ethnic, national and even international. In case of Indians, concept of identity is emotionally loaded.   This is because individuality is discouraged culturally; and, because their modus operandi revolves around being invisible & emotionally detached.

Indian identity is uniquely different from the Western identity. The western identity evolved in the context of religious persecution and use of confrontation and violence to be seen by others as "tough", in control and not vulnerable. Western identity seeks personal space and social control i.e. colonies or settlements. Whereas the origin and growth of Hindu/Indus civilization is rooted in spirituality – a universal sense of oneness and an extreme desire to de-emotionalize life. The approach to power struggle and control, for Indians, is carried out within – psychologically and not externally. It is one of the reason why India's philosophical psychologies are minimally religious and it is more of a science to decipher the nature of self, the human mind, personality, emotions and sustaining contentment. The idealism inherent in Hindu identity is a major pillar.

The "turmeric-anization" of the West has been a well-recognized phenomenon while, at the same time, India is going through Americanization. This sort of cultural amalgamation is nothing new. The entire world had populations moved around for various reasons: natural catastrophes, persecutions, missionaries, slavery, indentured labor, invaders, traders, Europeans seeking new territories, and wars have continued to globalize and yet, at the same time, fragment societies.

Identity is multidimensional and not just based on passport, religion or the country of birth. It is not as simple as defining individuals in terms of "pure", "full blooded" and straight forward packages. Indians have diverse physical characteristics ranging from mongoloid, Caucasoid to Negroid features. Many have married across castes, religions, provinces and races. Biracial children among Indians living abroad are a significant population. It's also not uncommon that couples follow different religions while living in the same household. Indians born abroad do not speak any of the Indian languages but identify themselves as Indian. They carry out Hindu rituals in Sanskrit without understanding the meanings. It all raises the question as to who is an Indian or what is an Indian identity. Some can accept and live without answering the question but the majority of people need to feel part of something bigger, to have a special bond to a psychological homeland.

Identity formation begins in childhood. Of course, it's never perfect for anyone but being raised by a village is always better than growing up in in an uncertain, unpredictable, insecure, erratic social milieu with confused values. It can be distressing if early upbringing is traumatic and/or role modeling is dysfunctional. Elaborate speeches or explanations do not work with children. They need to learn from seeing. Caring and simple structures provide a sense of safety to the children. Children are not mini-adults but are simply children with their own unique needs, limitations and psychology. Adolescence, on the other hand, is a particularly challenging phase where the need to be comfortable with oneself becomes all consuming. If they are bullied, ashamed of their family, resentful of their culture and full of self-doubts about their own pigmentation and physical characteristics, they may suffer from identity crisis. If one's identity is in crisis, what is left to build on? This crisis may show by their tenacious condemning everything Indian from language, religion, food and even their own Indian name, or by starting to abuse drugs/alcohol and exhibiting a decline in school performance. Self-destructive risk-taking, mental breakdown or depression or suicide can also occur.

In the article titled "Values of Indian and American Adolescents", Sundberg, Rohila, and Tyler (1970) compared the values of Indian and American adolescents. They concluded that Indian lives center around family, with an emphasis on deference, conformity, and external control. This is in contrast to Americans, where the emphasis is on sensuous enjoyment, religiosity, and sociability.

Adulthood does not spare individuals the implication of identity related issues. A person with conflicted identity does not only fail to realize his/her full potential but fails to fulfill required related role-related, work, academic and social responsibilities. The balancing act between what one is, what is required of one and what can realistically be delivered is a major stressor. Indians struggle with opposing demands from significant others and often fail to properly prioritize and thus lose everyone in the process.

A healthy identity is rooted in being grounded in one's own sense of individuality, clear awareness as to the boundaries, clarity as to one's values, and the ability to perform in different roles without confusion, ambivalence, and undue stress. Becoming a health personality is a process and requires openness of mind to learn/grow and, above all, the recognition of the importance of feelings/emotions.

Before identifying Indian values, it's necessary to evaluate the context of the need to identify the dilemmas dealing with Indian Identity issues. It's a positive thing in terms of the western culture that a person from childhood onward is encouraged, nurtured and rewarded to be an individual in their own right rather than merely an extension of a family or a carbon copy of parents. In contrast, Indians reward total compliance, obedience, loyalty to the family and being an extension of the extended family. The model child, in the Indian context, is merely the one who emulates his parents and other elders.

The support for the individual's uniqueness is precious to the western mind. The greater the uniqueness of the Indian child, the greater the threat to the Indian family and community. In other words, conformity is synonymous with the Indian notion of identity. By and large, Indians while young, have to operate on two levels i.e. the external being conformist while internally, and often secretly, entertaining his or her own unique ambitions, aspirations, dreams and fantasies. Indian parents need to understand the necessity of the individual to distance and separate self in healthy ways and also to engage in trial and error in order to find oneself.

Indians need not become frightened. Parents should make genuine attempts on their own or seek professional help to manage their often subjective and exaggerated fears and panic.

Parents should stop being barriers and should instead facilitate child and adolescent individuality, creativity and self-acceptance in order to prevent feeling split and confused.

Home cannot offer everything a child needs to develop a healthy identity. Interaction with neighbors, peers and with the larger world is absolutely essential. Parents can play a positive role in promoting and facilitating such experiences and in turn use them as an opportunity for their own growth as well. Children are the best teachers for the immigrant Indian diaspora.

- Identity formation is a process and cannot be demanded, imposed or dictated. A person may try out various versions of it, only to eventually find a balance and grounding. The process should not be obstructed but definitely managed carefully to prevent any serious risk taking behaviors like drugs, unsafe sex or criminal acting out.
- Identity as clung to by Indians born in India, makes them expect unrealistic responses from others i.e. "straight line" behavior. Examples of straight-line behavior are education-job-marriage-parental responsibilities – simultaneously fulfilling all other roles as a son/daughter, grandchild, sibling, etc. Indians' tolerance for a husband or wife having different religions, biracial children, intimacy with black or Spanish people, academically, socially or financially under-accomplished is dangerously absent because it does not fit straight line thinking. It needs self-confrontation and dropping holier than thou judgmental rigidity.
- Children should never be prejudiced against other cultural, ethnic and national groups or the country of adoption. They should be allowed to form their own impressions and negotiate on their own terms.
- Feeling split between one's culture of origin and adopted country is somewhat normal. However, it should be addressed in the spirit of "best of the both worlds "and all bias to see non-Indian things as inferior should be dropped in personal, community and work life.
- Unresolved identity issues have the potential to sabotage parenting, marriage, adjustment at work, leadership role and public image. Identity full of conflict and dysfunction can trigger mental problems and other abnormal habits.

The Dalai Lama, when asked what surprised him most about humanity, answered "Men. Because he sacrifices his health in order to make money. Then he sacrifices money to recuperate his health. And then he is so anxious about the future that he does not enjoy the present; the result being that he does not live in the present or the future; he lives as if he is never going to die, and then dies having never really lived."

Indian Values

Values are core of one's beliefs. These beliefs guide one's behavior and even emotions. It is extremely important for one to know one's belief system as well as realization that certain values are very sacred while others are open for revision and some do not even matter. Value clarification is part of psychological counseling.

Some values are universal. Murdering one's mother or children are universal taboos. Protecting women and children are universal ideals. Helping out the elderly is practiced in every culture. Values change through time. In the west, many decades ago, family used to the center of all social life and children were expected to be obedient, respectful and make sacrifices for significant others. However, since the post-world war era and with the growth of the capitalism, the family has become nuclear and marriages based on love. Need for personal space has become a necessity. In the Muslim and Christian countries one can marry one's second cousin. Hindus have to rule out the possibility of over 1100 blood relations before being able to get married with another person. Values are deeply held beliefs which determine behavior. A person believing in Ahinsa (non-injury) will be overwhelmed if required to eat meat. In the west, dominant belief is that fish and fowl are for men's consumption. Muslims consider a dog as a devil. Hindus fear cats and avoid them as pets. A person believing in patriotism has no choice but to see his country as superior. A religious fanatic has to practice his beliefs even if they are irrational and unproductive. Belief system covers every aspect of life from birth to death, food to health, self to others, money, power, pleasure, pain, sex, after death, life style to every choice one has to make. Life decisions depend upon beliefs. Confusion about values can become a major source of mental problems. Feeling uncertain as to what values are not open for examination, what are open for compromise and which ones are insignificant and do not matter can be a major stressor. Value clarification is often considered an important part of psychotherapy.

Psychotherapy facilitates individual identity and value examination to promote relevant and effectiveness in the context of "here and now".

The Hindu belief system is rather complex due to its being rooted in ancient culture, having evolved through the historical-political experiences, religious evolutions and globalization. Hindu philosophical psychologies have gone through major evolution because of reformers Sankracharya, like Buddha and Jain. Buddhists allow any food as determined by the context of time-place and person. Jains, no matter what, distance themselves even from honey, milk, and in-ground vegetables as they are considered injurious to other living things. At a visible level, in a rather overly simplistic manner, Hindu behavior is determined by the following values. It's an overly condensed version since a civilization like Indian cannot be reduced to merely a paragraph or page or two.

- In the hierarchy of things, an individual is subordinate to the family, which is subordinate to the community, which, in turn, is subordinate to the country and all of them combined are guided by the ideal of *Vasudaive Kutumbkam*, i.e. the world is one family. Individuals are expected to make personal sacrifices such as women separating from the family of origin at marriage, guests being given personal space and own needs suspended for children and elders. Role-modeling renders all Indians, no matter what their place in the family or society, responsible for adopting model ethics, morality, simplicity, wisdom, modesty and other virtues. As a result, the predominant mode of learning for Hindus is observational learning, rather than trial and error as is prevalent in the West.
- Obedience to the chronologically older person, higher in hierarchy, or the person who is wise, scholarly, or has seniority is very commendable and commonplace. This is in contrast to the West, where individuality, independence, even of a child, is given a priority.
- Self-worth is defined from inside and also based on one's sacrifices and character traits, unlike in the West, where many use external benchmarks such as income, appearance, height, sex appeal and possessions such as car, house, wardrobe, etc.
- Indians establish friendships for the sake of friendships, and it does not have to be based on ulterior motives such as sex, money, hobby, religion, work or need. It is not unique to Indians since Arabs, Africans, Spanish and most Asians idealize the same value system.

- The Indian concept of space is very loose, broad, and flexible almost to the point of being non-existent. As a result of Indians' openness to personal, psychological and even physical space, they feel no need for boundaries even at the cost of being negatively stereotyped.
- Non-reactivity over reacting is deeply entrenched in Indian psyche. As a result, Indians are often seen as unresponsive, passive, not engaged, or self-absorbed due to their not reacting, delayed reaction or subjective action.
- Indians define themselves via the family, caste, region they belong to instead of religion, nation or individuality.
- Indians experience themselves through their roles and responsibilities i.e. son, sibling, cousin, father, spouse or their vocation/profession.
- Unlike in the past when money, materialism, possessions, display of wealth was considered as immodest and un-Indian, now the shift is in juxtaposition. Money has become an important tool for social acceptance.

Psycho-Pathology in the Diaspora

Psycho-pathology means the interplay of forces within the person as well as external variables. Sigmund Freud talked about interplay between id, ego, and super-ego while Thomas Harrison used the terminology to describe psychological interplay, "child, adult, and parent". Hindu psychology (Sankhya, Vedanta) has its own terminology, concepts, and personality structure which are very different from Western psychology. However, the Western context is being utilized in the book due to the Diaspora being dispersed all over the world.

Pathological deviations from normal behavior are a relatively recent phenomenon among the Indian Diaspora population. It may have always existed but did not enter into the social discussion or receive media attention. The *Catch a Predator* show on NBC had at least three Indian cases of adult, married men trying to engage minors in sex. Ethnic newspapers are replete with news of Indians engaging in white collar crimes, suicides, murder-suicides, violent acting out, DUI as well as other crimes. My reviews of some of this news pointed towards mental illness such as bipolar disorder, addictions and personality disorders.

As such, research is sketchy as to the epidemiology of mental illness, suicides & institutionalizations, etc. There is even a greater lack of research as to how to effectively diagnose or treat abnormal behaviors among Indians. At the same time, the toolkit (Test batteries and treatment procedures) used by Western mental health professionals will not work with this population unless it is modified to meet this group's unique needs. Reliability and validation of these tests are also an issue. Even if the toolkit is modified, practitioners confront an array of cultural obstacles that can interfere with effective treatment. Obstacles include denial, avoidance, a lack of information and education, arrogance, guardedness, and pseudo-pride. Fear of change due to unfamiliarity, and avoidance of feelings due to fear of becoming overwhelmed are also common defenses among many.

Cultural Obstacles

Culture conveys the essence of one's geo-psycho-socio-somoto-econo-political aspects of personality. Human beings learn to organize their behavior in response to their culture. They respond to the events, process information, and often react based on their cultural biases.

One's definition of self, others, and the world is usually processed based on one's specific cultural background. The influence of religion as well as personal variables also play an important part.

For Indian Diaspora residents in poorer countries, the main obstacles to optimal mental health are not cultural, but economic handicaps, lack of resources, and a mental health information void. Aside from not having access to mental health providers, they simply do not know how to label/verbalize the problem they're experiencing and from whom to seek help.

In affluent countries like U.S.A., Canada, UK, and Australia, the obstacles are cultural and mostly involve extreme stigma attached to seeking treatment for any non-physical ailment. Denial is the first defense against the anxiety of having a mental health problem. Samir, an Indian friend, who has lived in the USA for 12 years summarized the stigma as follows:

> *"The term 'mental health' to Indians means either 'normal' or 'crazy.' By that definition, not seeing a mental health professional is 'normal.' Very few understand that treating mental issues is a science of behavior management. The social stigma of going to a mental health professional is very high (as high as having a sexual disease), and results in social rejection and branding."*

Some additional observations:

- Indians come from a strong religious and superstitious background where misery is karmic and one must surrender to it. Emotional equanimity is in essence the core of Hindu mental health.
- The social stigma articulated above results in sweeping problems under the rug, i.e. denial.
- Loss of face and social humiliation continue to result in the avoidance of seeking help, sometimes with devastating consequences.
- Immigrant Indians display a sort of competitiveness which negatively impacts them when it comes to dealing with marital, intergenerational, addiction, and mental health issues.
- Indians often believe that their unique cultural, religious, and national background makes them immune to human weaknesses and emotional disorders. This causes a great deal of avoidance, noncompliance, and self-sabotage.
- Indians are often averse to having to pay for mental health services.

- When Indians get in trouble, they often attempt to seek out all sorts of shortcuts to get out of trouble, thus they do not take advantage of the crisis to confront the deeper issue.
- Hindus view feelings as things to be suppressed, repressed, and brought under the control. This leaves them vulnerable to eventually acting out and losing of control of repressed feelings.
- Due to social and family structure, defined roles, and the pecking order described earlier, it is next to impossible for junior members to confront older family members. Similarly, wives do not feel that they have a legitimate authority to confront, therefore preventing the enabling of behavior is next to impossible.
- Talking is not the normal Indian mode of communicating, making it harder for mental professionals to gather data, process the information, or effectively intervene.
- Silence, depression, and turning anger and fear inward come easily to Indians due to cultural practices and values. Silently suffering is second nature to Indians. Hindus view suffering as a result of karmic factors which one has no control of, so why bother?

Indians frequently express complaints about falling victim to political exploitation, intimidation at work, and relationship conflicts or tension with neighbors. They often view illness or injury as caused by what "karmically" happens to the body, as opposed to something that is within their control. It is ingrained in the collective unconscious of Hindus that as long as one has a body, suffering is inevitable and acceptance, surrender, and silence are the proper responses.

- Self-blame is habitually utilized either in the name of bad karma, not having done good deeds to earn right karma, or having failed in some other way. This renders helpless those who are in a position to help, confront or stop enabling the self-blame.
- Indians are phobic of separation and boundaries, and therefore continue to merge boundaries and pay a heavy price in terms of loss of freedom, autonomy, and assertion of individuality. Joint and extended family are manifestations of this tradition to keep the family together and discourage any individuation. The phenomenon continues even after immigration, at the very high cost of depression, conflicts, and interpersonal damage.
- Self-sacrifice is in the core of Hindu family order. In spite of it being an overrated response, it often drives interpersonal behavior.
- Contradictions, paradoxes, and hypocrisies are accepted as part of the "big picture" of things that do not need to be resolved.

In essence, the psycho-dynamics of the Hindu Indian individual is closely tied to the family and community at large. The complexity interferes with objectively looking at the problem and finding efficient, immediate, and direct solutions. Indirectly, it delays the diagnosis, getting help in time and results in difficult to manage multi-layered co-morbid issues.

Suicide

In India, some 100,000 people per year commit suicide, at rates that have been steadily increasing for the past two decades. Although there are no comprehensive statistics, indications are that suicide rates or attempted suicide rates are also increasing in Diasporic countries, particularly the UAE, Britain, Trinidad, Malaysia, and Fiji.

- In the last two decades, the suicide rate in India has increased from 7.9 to 10.3 per 100,000.
- Studies of women in the South Asian Diaspora suggest that married women in immigrant communities are more vulnerable and at risk for suicide than native women. These studies reveal a strong link between marital and family problems and a wide range of health problems among Indians overseas.
- According to a 1996 study conducted by S.P. Patel and A.C. Gaw of the Department of Psychiatry, Boston University Medical Center Hospital, "suicide rates of young women immigrants from the Indian subcontinent are consistently higher than those of their male counterparts and of young women in the indigenous populations of the countries to which they immigrate."
- Patel and Gaw (1996) found that family conflict appeared to be the precipitating factor in many suicides, and that mental illness was rarely cited as the cause.
- A Malaysian study by S. Ong and Y.K. Leng reported that among residents of Kuala Lumpur, Indians form 10% of the population but account for 30% of suicides and 48% of attempted suicides.
- Although there are no comprehensive statistics, numerous reports have indicated high rates of suicides of Indian expatriates in Gulf countries. In Oman, official 2012 data indicated that one Indian commits suicide every six days, reportedly because of financial distress or personal issues. K. V. Shamsudheen, Chairman of the Pravasi Bandhu Welfare Trust in the UAE, said that high rates of suicides among unskilled and semi-skilled NRIs in the Gulf are often prompted by a financial crisis resulting from the vast gap between soaring expectation and ground reality.

- Suicide has been ranked as the leading cause of death among South Asians ages 15–24 in the United States
- Death and suicidal ideation rates for the macro elderly Asian American group (which includes Indian Americans) seeking primary care are higher than for any other racial group.

General risk factors for suicide in any population are past psychiatric history and present symptoms (depression, schizophrenia, alcohol dependency, and psychopathic personality), social factors (isolation, unemployment), and past history of suicide attempts. Risk factors for suicide attempts include recent attempts, precautions taken to avoid discovery, prior communication of suicidal intent, and the completion of final acts in anticipation of death.

Among Indians in India, psychosocial stressors leading to suicide include difficulties in cultural assimilation, inter-generational conflicts, interracial and interreligious marriages, divorce, gender role conflicts, and the younger generation feeling misunderstood and unsupported by parents. Among Diaspora Indians, the immigration factor complicates the picture and challenges Indians coping mechanism since extended families are absent, support systems are limited, and traditional values and solutions are less available.

Suicide is very threatening, disruptive and a very final act and yet it has existed in every society, religion, culture since the beginning of time. It is not about to disappear. Therefore society and particularly mental health professionals have a major obligation to detect it and help the person through the process of overcoming their internal suffering, external threats and, above all, relocate the purpose and direction in life. Therapeutic institutions must offer the "sanctuary" until the person regains his/her composure. Police have a primary obligation to abstain from further traumatizing or criminalizing the person or the family. Suicide is always a clinical matter unless one is in such a chronic, severe, intractable, hopeless pain secondary to disease like incurable cancer. An elderly person who feels that they have lost all dignity, autonomy, self-respect and chooses not to waste their money on the health systems' heroic efforts to keep them alive, should also be respected and allowed medically managed inexpensive suicide.

Some general thoughts:

- Bipolar disorder, manic depressive illness, and mood disorder play an important role in triggering suicidal behavior. As there may be a genetic component to these disorders, it is vital to know the family history and reasonable to suspect that the condition may have passed down from generation to generation.
- It is important to watch out for adolescent behavioral changes. If adolescents suddenly act different, see if stressors such as drug abuse or depression are the cause. As children are not always comfortable in talking directly, one may need to communicate subtly or involve a third party that has established a rapport with the child.
- Adult Indians living abroad in Western countries tend to be in high stress jobs, work long hours, and lack the cultural skills to be sensitive to adolescent feelings. They are more likely to miss the clues. Moreover, Indians operate based on unspoken expectations and have difficulty coping when these are not met. Their expectations can cause severe stress, anger, and depression, which can turn into suicidal behavior.
- Indian family life typically revolves around work and earning, professional success, and academic performance. Parents are hyper-focused on their own high achievement and their children obtaining good grades. Stresses inherent in this focus can build up and families may minimize the importance of stress as something that needs to be addressed.

The Diaspora in Crisis

*"When written in Chinese, the word "crisis" is composed of
two characters-one represents danger, and the other
represents opportunity."*

Crisis is not unique to Indians. For example, Jews have felt it, lived
through it and continue to face the aftermath and even ongoing
challenges to their existence. We all remember the killing fields of
Cambodia, the massacre in Rwanda and the genocide of the Native
Americans in the USA, Maoris in Australia, and many other crises.
Indians have had three golden eras but faced crisis when they lived in
pre-colonized India and then left the country as indentured labors for
the British, only to be betrayed when not provided with the return fare
that was part of their contract. They faced multiple challenges and
threats in their adopted countries, but managed to survive. Later,
immigrants to the West and other countries were more fortunate but the
challenges to personal mental health, parenting, marriage, and family
integrity have replaced the financial and survival crises. Diaspora
Indians in non-Western or non-developed countries and islands
continue to suffer from political, social, and financial threats.

Indian Diaspora individuals – whether in Fiji, Suriname, Ghana, Kenya,
or in the UK, Canada, or the U.S – metaphorically are "Indians out of
India without India being out of them." They may become flexible
enough to consume alcohol socially, eat meat, and attempt to adapt to
the mainstream, but deep down inside they are grounded in Indian
values. This means that family defines them as individuals, and that
they are required to conform to family expectations at almost any cost.
Other ingrained values include the expectation of loyalty to the family
hierarchy, seeing the goal of Moksha (freedom from it all), seeing
attachment as the source of suffering, and practicing religion quietly,
privately, without loud displays or proselytizing others.

Indian roles and responsibilities are defined by hierarchy. The older
generation and their dependencies are respected unconditionally and
their advice and wisdom is sought after. Children are expected to build
character, play, pursue education, and respect family tradition. The
middle generation is supposed to provide for all the extended family,
enhance respect for the family and the name of their forefathers,
empower the family to face any crisis, and meet all the challenges of
social and financial obligations.

This system has worked rather successfully for Indians for the past 10,000 plus years, and has sustained Hindu civilization and minimized family disintegration in the face of tumultuous national history of foreign aggression. It has not only kept the Diaspora connected with Mother India but also fended Indians from mental disorders, addictions, perversions, and crime. The Ashram system (described in a later chapter), the Hindu age-based social system which defines the four stages of life, has proved itself to be one of the best known mental hygiene prescriptions for allowing Indians to understand the purpose, priorities, and goals in life.

Dhruv was the son of the first Queen Suniti. King Uttanapada's second wife Suruchi also had a son, and she was determined to see that her own son became the next King, rather than Dhruv. Dhruv, being the older son, was entitled to be the King. Suruchi exiled Dhruv and his mother to the forest, away from the royal palace. When Dhruv asked his mother who his father was, the queen replied that he was the Great King Uttanapada. Dhruv left the house feeling hurt and went into the forest to meditate. There were Seven Sages who were also meditating nearby. They meditated together, and soon God Vishnu noticed the strength of Dhruv's meditation and asked what he desired. Dhruv smiled silently, God Vishnu then turned Dhruv into "The Pole Star", surrounded by bright stars around.

The Indian social system was relatively intact until the Islamist takeover by Babur on Feb 14th, 1483 when, under external mortal threat, it retracted, hibernated, and isolated itself. The influence of the British Raj (1600-1947) further damaged the Indian psyche, collective pride, and the family's ability to function as an open and independent institution. In more recent times, the following factors have created a different sort of crisis, i.e. a mental health crisis:

- Increased social, financial, and emotional complexity has arisen due to new variables such as globalization, commercialization, and consumerism.
- In the U.S. increased amounts of Indian wealth have resulted in parallel expansions in Western-style consumption. This has negatively altered the centrality of the family and its integration within community.
- Emigration and cross-cultural exposure and the need to assimilate or adapt has thrown Indians into confusion and stress that they are not equipped to handle due to lack of experience and background.

- The trend is that the younger generation is eager to sever the "umbilical cord" at an earlier age. This results in separating, individuating, and engaging in "trial and error" behaviors, searching for autonomy and adulthood.

Indian traditions used to serve a useful mental health maintenance role but are now being let go. For example, the custom was that married women returned to their parents' house in the rainy season (saawan). This allowed an acceptable regression to the girl role and distance from the stress of being a wife, mother, and daughter-in-law. It also promoted sharing and catharsis with the childhood peer group. Similarly, events which have therapeutic value, such as Bhaiya Dauj (Brother's Day) and Holi, the spring religious festival, are losing their appeal.

> "Freud refers to 'desexualized' energy with reference to sublimation, in which case the drive is hindered from forming sexual object cathexes that might be dangerous (with a parent, for instance), and is reoriented to a non-sexual goal. Accordingly, desexualized energy will eventually discharge itself as writing, religious worship, art, or music, among other cultural, intellectual, or even sporting, pursuits."

The best and the most unique aspect of Indian culture was its understanding and deep grounding in the culture of sublimation. A Hindu child early on knew that there is no room for sexuality, alcohol, drugs, or wasteful leisure time. One was supposed to direct all his or her energy towards character building, rising above the mundane, and accomplishing extraordinary feats through creativity, spirituality, religiosity, or learning.

Now that it is all changing fast, Indians are stuck in a time warp and face new and unfamiliar challenges. As a consequence, Indians are showing their distress through depression, OCD, academic failures, suicide-homicide, psychosis, PTSD, anxiety disorders, manic-depression, personality disorders, and increasingly acting out through criminal behaviors. Alcohol and drug addictions are also emerging as threats. The Diaspora is not equipped and lacks any networking or resources to survive the threat to mental health that affects marriage, family, parenting and care for the older generation. It is undergoing a crisis unparalleled to any other time in the history of Indian civilization.

Apathy as the Root of Crisis

By some measures, it appears as though Indian Diaspora communities are doing quite well and are viewed as a modern minority. India is one of the world's fastest growing economies. In just under two decades, it has become a global force in software, outsourcing, R&D, and high-tech manufacturing. Indians in the USA are the wealthiest among all of the Diaspora, and have the highest college graduation rates of all ethnic groups; contribute a disproportionately large number of engineers, IT workers, and physicians. Some of the country's corporate giants, including Microsoft, HP, IBM, and Pepsico, have Indians in top leadership positions.

On the other hand, in the non-Western Diaspora, many of its citizens are victims of discrimination, terror, murder, sexual violence, forced conversions, and ethnic cleansing, as documented in the 2011 HAF Report.

On a psychological level, the major causes of this crisis are the malaise of Hindu apathy and a collective feeling of inferiority towards the West. The apathy is the reason that, despite undeniable successes, Indians lack any systematic approach to addressing mental health needs, preventing social pathologies, and collectively addressing issues that affect the community. The sense of inferiority can be seen in the pervasive Indian denial and disavowal of Hindu heritage, despite the widespread re-appropriation, and mass-marketing of Hindu-influenced practices such as yoga, meditation, and fasting.

A prevalent stereotype is that Hindus are categorized as submissive, acquiescent, consenting, passive, and have an unhealthy tendency to tolerate abusive behavior. This negative image has portrayed Indians as easy targets for exploitation, manipulation, and victimization by interest groups ranging from corporations to proselytizers. The irony is that Hindus do not see the ground realities, changing demography, and the challenges to Hindu identity that threaten their existence.

Psychologically speaking, Hindus behave according to Hindu thinking, which is a combination of concepts, values, and beliefs. A Hindu wakes up praying for the well-being of the entire creation, practices non-injury, believes that all religions are as good as his own, and defines the entire world as one big family. As a result, Hindus, because of their vocabulary and concepts, fail to confront adversity and process reality objectively. Hindu apathy for their own feelings and the outcomes of neglecting them has thus become a defense mechanism for Hindus to escape into their own imaginary cocoon and mask depression, anxiety, and fear. What's masked is neither owned nor decisively acted upon. Bhagwata Gita is known to prescribe actions without anticipations and expectations.

The Hindu concept of ego is a double-edged sword. On the one hand, because of the belief that ego is the cause of all suffering the Hindu projects apathy, indifference, detachment, and self-deprecation. The purpose of life is seen as Moksha, which requires systematic depletion and eventual destruction of the ego; letting go of the ego is seen as a prerequisite for good mental health as it inoculates one from narcissism, personalization, and doom and gloom. On the other hand, this concept if taken to the extreme, risks self-degradation. What's needed is a balanced perspective that acknowledges the need for a healthy and productive ego applicable to changing contexts in life.

The evolution of the Indian personality and national character has rarely been examined in the context of collective Hindu experience through history. The traditional Indian mental hygiene solutions, which were once easily available and culturally pervasive, are now lost, defunct or have no appeal. The breakdown of the social-family-community network has been in the making since the invasions of the Muslims and British. The extended family has been under assault, and it is also losing its traditional role as insurance against all odds and circumstances. This is the last straw and if the trend is not reversed then Indian society will change to an unrecognizable entity.

Western approaches to mental health diagnosis and treatment are not congruent, relevant in their entirety, or easily applicable to Indian populations due to the contextual, core personality and conceptual differences. Indians tend to not utilize formal mental health services such as psychotherapy, group sessions, and outpatient programs. Their rationalization, denial, sublimation, and attempting to cope by suffering in silence is a deterrent to becoming a consumer of mental health.

This is despite the fact that Western mental health practices have made remarkable progress and contributions to human happiness. The U.S. in particular has been the leader in applying the principles of psychology to the needs of the masses. For Indians, an ideal solution will be to blend the best of Hindu psychology and Western psychology.

Family Dynamics

The Indian family unit operates like a tribe. It is rooted in biological, hierarchical, predetermined roles and responsibilities, all living under one roof and bound by unconditional loyalty. Anything that threatens the family structure – modernization, change, entry, and exits from the unit – is viewed as a crisis. Separations, divorce, conversion, and marrying outside the tradition are all taboos. Any one member's failure, betrayal, lethargy, or ineptitude is capable of triggering dysfunction and disintegration of the family.

The sons are the vehicles for the stability of the family and therefore every affair of their lives is micro-managed from birth until death. Daughters are brought up to get married and join their husbands' families, not only physically but emotionally and in terms of total loyalty. The sons' roles are complex, multiple and vital for the sustenance of the extended family. Even after getting married and having his own children, a man is expected to remain primarily a son, a brother, a cousin, and only then a father and husband. It's not hard to imagine that the burden sons carry and the sacrifices wives make are extraordinary, which is nothing less than cultural martyrdom.

The context of puppy love, dating, and living in common law arrangement is entirely different from the reality of the marriage. Healthy marriages arranged or based on love require honed, direct, open, blunt contractual understanding and agreeing about issues and values of sexual intercourse, parenting, handling in-laws, money matters, future directions and, above all, management of anger, fear, panic, worrying, jealousy, and other negative feelings. "Love" is not good enough to guarantee happiness or harmony. Premarital counseling is a cost-effective measure to prevent unnecessary suffering and pain. Sex before marriage dilutes the sanctity of marriage. Dowry, domestic violence, and infidelity have no place in a healthy marriage. Happy marriages require two individuals feeling complete and then coming together rather than morbid clinging, dependency or expecting the other partner to make them feel good, secure or whole.

Children are brought up tenderly and every female in the family plays the maternal role. The queen mother in the family can be a mother or grandmother, who tends to be a benign dictator who keeps everyone in line. She has favorites: first born sons, grandsons, granddaughters, daughters, elderly and only then daughter-in-laws. She herself makes sacrifices for everyone and does not usually have double standards, i.e. treating herself with special benefits or goodies. The grandfather tends to be on the sidelines and barely involved (see the later section, *The Elderly*).

As overwhelming and stressful as this structure may seem, it has served Indians well. Compare the Indian family to those in any other culture or country and it uniquely stands out in terms of producing disciplined children, fewer or no delinquent adolescents, law-abiding citizens, and societies that respect its adults like divinity. It has kept up the integrity of marriage and the sanctity of children being born and reared by both biological parents under the guidance of elders. The Indian family to date has the most evolved "cousin culture," i.e., no matter where they live or how long it has been since they've seen one another, the "cousins" maintain an intimate bond based on mutual respect.

The traditional Indian family has gone through serious jolts within the past 1,100 years and is undergoing dramatic changes, not necessarily all positive. This has the potential risk of diluting everything Indian, from relational loyalties, passing of the cultural traditions to the next generation, as well as the language, food, and music, which are crucial to sustain one's unique identity. With the extinction of the Indian extended family tradition, the death of India as we know her is inevitable to follow. There is no substitute for it. Change is inevitable but its haste and suddenness – due to urbanization, capitalism, materialism, consumerism, westernization, and hyper-individualistic orientation – is creating irreparable alienation, confusion, and social and emotional pathology.

The decay of the Indian family is obvious, visible through the increase in sibling rivalries, promiscuity, rape, alcoholism, vehicular homicides and violence, all of which were previously not pervasive behaviors. The impact of confusion and alienation will soon become clear through an escalating trend of higher number of divorces, domestic violence, adultery, premarital pregnancies, depression, suicides, murders, and addictions.

The older generation is in crisis as well, feeling deaf, mute, dumb, blind and powerless due to the rapid loss of the familiar and having nothing better to replace it. Diaspora has not come up with a viable solution. The elderly lack the skills to be autonomous. On the other hand, they fail to recognize the distress of the younger generation feeling sandwiched under the load of expectations from everybody. The elderly live by the old ideals of expecting the younger generation to be the

"Shravan Kumar," the mythical Indian son who exhibited unparalleled devotion toward his parents, sacrificing everything personal. The days of collective sharing of resources, personal space, and extended family as meeting all needs of every member are gone forever. Family in the 21st century cannot continue to be the unconditional sanctuary for every generation and every significant other. In other words, there is no choice but to incorporate the values of self-dependency, individual responsibility and timely planning.

Husbands

The husband is in the center of most actions by virtue of being a son; he is expected to be depended upon for safety, security, resources, compliments, comfort, and solutions. He is not at the top of the hierarchy but his central location in the order is vital due to his productivity and insurance value. Everybody wants a piece of him and his roles are so diverse that often he lives in the state of mini-breakdown (duress) and waits for bliss either through emigration, relocation, or if lucky, having parents who prefer their own autonomy, an occurrence that happens infrequently.

The Indian husband feels that his first obligation and duty is to his parents and siblings and only then to his children and wife. One of the major causes of marital conflicts in Indian Diaspora is when the wife is not able to or willing to follow the traditional protocol and instead demands control, attention, solicits power to run her house her way. When the hierarchies are bypassed, the extended family fails to function. Most husbands operate on the basis of cultural assumptions that everybody, including their spouses, will surrender to the expected traditional roles and protocols. They do not feel the need to address these issues and often fail to renegotiate expectations. The Mahabharata of conflicts and power struggles become unmanageable when unresolved marital issues spill over on other significant others and in-laws. This naiveté and attitude of assumptions can potentially jeopardize the future of marriage and at the very least, peace of mind for years to come. There are no winners.

The Indian character trait of not openly verbalizing and negotiating expectations with parents, spouses, significant others and family relatives, friends, guests and visitors often plays havoc with lasting consequences. Indians, male or female, characteristically operate on assumptions borrowed from traditions and culture. They anticipate, as well as expect, that others will understand them. This pattern is deeply rooted in the Indian personality because of the preference to avoid confrontation at any cost, and also not to be open with their agendas and ulterior motives. This character defect is not malicious, but simply a learned behavior to take the easy way out from any possibility of confrontation.

Another major stressor Indian husbands experience is rooted in their family expectations as well their self-imposed need to ensure the settling of their siblings. This role revolves around financially providing for their education, seeking employment, and even negotiating their marriages. This sacrifice often tends to be one sided, due to the idealistic need to be a positive role model and to prove his loyalty while expecting parental admiration. Wives notice this parasitic or abusive pattern, but the husbands lack skills to question or confront their siblings. Wives' protests prove futile, often resulting in anger and marital conflicts as husbands expect them to surrender and acquiesce. The complaining does not stop, in spite of its futility. Typically, the intention is to protect the nuclear family's financial resources; the husband should "wise up," see the game, and renegotiate the boundaries. Here again, the expected loyalty to siblings becomes a genuine source of abuse, misuse, and aggravation, impacting negatively on the marriage.

Also, Indian husbands see their paternal families and all their clan members as superior to the in-laws' family, while the wife's family is considered lower in the hierarchy. Their expected behavior is to shower the husband's family with gifts, recognition, and self-sacrifice. In recent times, Indian wives have become aware of these dynamics and desire equality and freedom from traditional expectations. However, in the interim, it remains a significant source of marital conflict. The essential dynamics of Indian husbands revolves around meeting complex unspoken expectations of parents, siblings, spouses, children, and the extended family.

As a consequence, a husband's separation, differentiation, individuation, and in essence being himself is not an option, at least during Grahastha phase of life. In this context, it is easy to understand that assertiveness, decisiveness, taking charge, confronting expectations, and communicating clearly are all very difficult for him. His fear is that the balance will be disturbed, creating a ripple in the status quo that will leave him too paralyzed to regain control. Husbands fear exposure, and find safety in being private, subtle, and indirect, even at the cost of losing credibility and creating a negative image. Indian wives feel dismissed and perceived as incompetent adults by their husbands. They often complain that their husbands do not understand their side, or advocate for them, and fail to support their emotional needs. This interplay exposes the conflicts, leading to vulnerability and potential confrontation. This behavioral pattern of passivity is the most common defense mechanism utilized to shield oneself from any threat, both internal and external.

Emotional Extortion

Indian husbands tend to be seen by their spouses as emotional scammers due to them acting as cultural robots, being emotionally apathetic and self-absorbed. On the other hand, in their other roles as sons, siblings, and fathers, they are devoted to perfection. In the husband role, men need to feel in control as they are preoccupied with parents needing care, guilt for not being there for their parents and siblings, and the dilemma of being in two countries at the same time. Simultaneously, they unwittingly complicate their stress as they do not discuss their dilemmas, agendas or feelings openly. They seek control by obsessing with money, ineffective attempts to control their spouse's income, pressuring them to live "simple," i.e. by expecting them not to be consumers, buy luxury items, finance emotional traveling (homesickness triggered visits) to India, and pressuring them not to send money to their own parents or siblings. Marital intimacy is lost due to struggles over money, fun, leisure time activities, and savings. In many marriages, husbands fail to define the financial situation realistically and thus remain rooted in unconscious insecurities and overcompensate by hoarding. Anecdotally, women are known to complain that men lack intimacy, emotional responsiveness, and tend to be self-absorbed. Self-absorption is a rather pervasive Indian personality trait. Husbands often

Individuals consult psychologists not just for mental illnesses but often to improve the quality of their "being", relationships, and to feel positive and live productive lives. These life goals are often sabotaged and complicated, mainly because people have no clear definition and act in a hit and miss fashion. Happiness is possible only when one has conceptual clarity, wakes up with a purpose, and then makes it happen. Happiness primarily is contentment, acceptance of life, living in the moment, being Satvik, integrating spirituality and balancing it with sensory pleasures. The importance of money is oversold. Intimacy, praying, playing, giving, simplicity, laughing, and being in the moment do not cost money. Self-imposed conditions like "bigger", "longer", "higher, "more", "greater", better" based on caparison with others and competitiveness are an miss, ignore, or dismiss wives' clues, verbalizations, emotions, and gestures as stressors. When the wife's behavior becomes very overt, she is perceived as adversarial, unreasonable, demanding and responsible for ruining the marriage. She is often shunned for being aggressive and causing shame to the family. When the husband's passivity becomes blatant and intolerable, the wife blames the husband for the cause of her depression and ruining the marriage. The gender psychology is different and often misunderstood universally. As a result, male and female relationships, especially in marriage, tend to be conflicted. Marriage therapists observe this phenomenon of pervasive dissatisfaction amongst spouses, causing unwarranted negative physical and emotional consequences involving finances, children, intimacy, and even suicide/homicide. For example, India Abroad reported on July 4, 2014, that a Michigan man was convicted of killing his wife and children. On February 7, 2014, a Florida mom killed her daughter and self.

Trishanku Syndrome

The Indian husband's state of mind can be metaphorically summarized as *Trishanku* – neither here nor there and perpetually in limbo. The phrase "Trishanku's heaven" is used widely in India to describe such situations/dilemmas faced in real life.

Trishanku is a character from the ancient Hindu literary tradition, and the phrase describes a middle-ground or a compromise between goals or desires and the current state. Trishanku is suspended in his own heaven as a compromise between the Earth that he belonged to and the heaven that he sought. He is hanging in heaven upside down.

Master of Defensiveness

Indian husbands more often than not will go to any lengths to avoid being confronted, even if constructively, because the realization of being imperfect, wrong, or needing to change is just too overwhelming. The rigidity and resistance is rooted in their lack of ability to identify feelings as well as appreciation to address. This trait includes not only self but significant others as well, i.e. being hyper focused on tasks and goals but not on feelings. They will abstain from professional help even if the cost is the loss of their marriage or their children's mental well-being.

As a psychologist, I have seen many marriages end in divorce even when the wife underwent treatment and made changes, wrote letters sharing very openly and constructively, and took most of the blame. In these instances, it is common for the husband to never respond, join therapy, or seek help for himself. Such defensiveness in the Indian character goes beyond husband-hood and is endemic in politicians, professionals, police, the court system, and all institutions.

Self-Absorption

Indians have the trait of hyper focusing on their own needs, agendas, and goals, which tends to sabotage the interpersonal interactions and outcomes. Taking things for granted comes naturally to them as it spares them from the responsibility of renegotiation of relationships to keep them afresh whether in business, marriage, or friendships.

Indian self absorption manifests itself in a rather pervasive personality trait of not verbalizing one's anticipations and expectations. Paradoxically, they assume that others must be aware of them. Very often, this results in risky consequences. One such example is that they tend to withhold any positive reinforcement and feedback, even if they internally appreciate it. This is rooted in the belief that one's "positive" actions are rewards in themselves. On the other hand, they are very quick to criticize or disapprove behaviors that do not meet the unspoken expectations. Thus, unlike in western cultures, Indians do not value nor utilize the power of positive reinforcement tools such as complements, rewards, tokens, affirmations or other such incentives.

Wives

The Indian wife is the person primarily responsible for passing on Indian values to future generations. She not only plays the role of a wife, but she is a mother, sister, daughter-in-law, and a friend, who for ages has been given the responsibility of preserving the religious and cultural values of India and preserving the "Indian-ness" in children. Although all the members of the family share the responsibility of protecting Indian values from getting distorted in the shadow of modern beliefs, it is the women of the house who most embody these responsibilities.

The status of Indian wives varies depending upon the husband's order of birth, his success and contribution to the extended family, the size of the family, expectations of the significant others, and how many female siblings are still unmarried and living at home.

In the scheme of things, the husband's mother has queen status, the husband's sisters stand second, and the Indian wife comes in third. In other words, wives live in an "on hold" status, like a woman in waiting for recognition, reprieve, peace of mind, and some sanity. A New Jersey housewife married for 20 years summarizes her feelings as follows:

> *After going through all possible psychological changes and different family circumstances, I realized in the end that I am still not in the position to distinguish my duties to myself and my duties towards the family. I am torn apart between trying to find my own individuality and my responsibilities and duties dictated to me by society and parents. Being told since childhood that I should find the happiness in 'giving' to the family, I never developed my ability to receive or accept any natural feelings, this includes sexual pleasure also.*

A wife's status and place are also determined by her own background, i.e. whether she comes from an influential/rich family, her level of education, whether she came with an adequate dowry, and whether her parents went out of their way to accommodate the husband's family. The wife's status is also defined by her ability to be a team player, her competence in mediating or not getting involved in power struggles, and her proficiency as a house cleaner/cook/ caretaker of elderly family members. In Indian society, the biggest impact of feminism has been on women in the spousal role asserting their individuality based on Western, particularly American, expectations.

The wife's most important allies are her mother-in-law and sister(s)-in-law. The wife of the oldest son is highest in the pecking order. It is important to note that the couple's intimacy and sexual needs are secondary to the business of taking care of the family. In other words, wives probably have the same amount of stress, exhaustion, and challenges as the husbands have in their multiple roles as sons, siblings, fathers and providers of the clan. While the husband can walk away to work or commiserate with friends, wives have fewer social outlets. Thus, mood shifts, depression, and psycho-somatic disorders are not uncommon.

After marriage, the bride traditionally moves to her husband's house, leaving behind her parental home and the memories of her childhood to lead an entirely new and different life. This is the biggest sacrifice she makes in her life, causing her to compromise her personal dreams and desires. Perhaps more than in other cultures, the emotion of sacrifice is recognized and revered. Indian brides are famous for demonstrating the values of forgiveness and sacrificing for the benefit of the family.

The following are characteristics that are common to most wives, but especially to Indian wives:

- Loyalty to Husband: An Indian wife sustains a deep loyalty with or without love for her husband. This stems from tradition, religion, and upbringing and is not always feeling based.
- Home is her castle: In wife role, an Indian woman is fully cognizant of the necessity, importance and the long term impact as to the dynamics of home culture. Everyone's mental health depends upon how harmonious and peaceful the home base is.
- Commitment to tradition and continuity of culture: In wife role, she is obligated, empowered and privileged to enrich the family with the proper nourishment, promoting the pursuit of spirituality and keeping the family glued. She is unmistakably the builder and protector of Indian tradition.
- Honoring Family Customs: She follows the family customs, keeps the traditions, and emerges as the empowered specialist as the facilitator of the rituals and samskaras.
- Readiness for Marriage: The Indian wife grows up with full awareness since childhood as to her role as a wife. Typically, she adapts herself to her husband, his family and their traditions, and to whatever circumstances life thrusts upon her. Personal individuality and need for boundaries are not viewed as significant. Traditionally it worked rather well. However, wife role now has become very stressful and the pressures to work, rear children, run households and also to care for significant others of her own and her husband's side of the family.

Children

Indian parents do not see their children as equals but at the bottom of the totem pole. This is not because they see children as unimportant, but because the social structure of Indian society is hierarchical. This is not seen as a negative but conducive for children to evolve, learn observationally, grow, accomplish, look up to their elders, and earn their medals. Particularly in Hindus, the belief is that the "ego," "I," "me," and "mine" must be depleted or suspended as a prerequisite to becoming wise, learned, and mature. That is one of the reasons children are not expected to have an ego or even an illusion that they are unique, special, or entitled to extraordinary privileges.

Children are provided for, protected, inspired, and loved rather deeply. This expression of love is often less verbal compared to Westerners. Indian parents tend not to be verbose, repetitive, or go overboard in letting the child know he is loved. It's not the giving of cakes, sneakers, clothes, gifts, or compliments which are equated with love, but rather the family sharing, mutual sacrifices of personal comforts, soft tone of voice, tender looks, inspiration, and exposure to opportunities.

Children of Indian Diaspora tend to have a clear awareness of their home culture in contrast to the mainstream majority culture. They are exposed to the differences at school, on playgrounds, and through their interactions with their peers. By and large, most kids are comfortable with this duality and rarely display any inferiority about being Indian. However, they are aware of being different not only in terms of physical appearance, but in their awareness that their families expect them to achieve, accomplish, and surpass others. They complain of missing out on some of the liberties and fun that their peers have. However, by and large, they conform to the family discipline and expectations. They also tend to have a rather unique "cousin culture," which empowers them, regardless of where their cousins, extended family, or fellow Diasporians reside. The participation in the "cousin network" helps them laugh and share the paradoxes of life in cultural dissonance, and also allows them to give and receive mentoring and counseling.

I have counseled numerous families. I also helped conduct a summer camp for Indian children, during which I asked them individually and in groups to discuss common issues. Although many of the themes outlined below are particularly relevant for U.S. Diaspora families, they likely echo issues experienced by Diaspora families worldwide.

- Indian children often complain that their parents micro-manage their behavior and that all of their time is watched, supervised, and controlled. This extreme over protectiveness makes children yearn to be free but at the same time afraid of venturing too far. I have seen many adolescent, school and college students alike, have a mental breakdown over having to be on their own, even while living in college dormitories.
- Indian parents tend to raise the bar every time a child is successful instead of celebrating the accomplishment.
- Indian parents' communication styles tend to be "preachy" or sermonizing, and make repeated references as to "how it was back in the old days." This is a subtle expectation game Indian parents'

play which make children feel put down, ashamed, and confused as to their cultural identity.

- Children are not encouraged to express opinions and share feelings. These feelings, both repressed and suppressed, can have dire consequences, from depression to suicide.
- Indian parents lack sensitivity as to the importance of peer interaction, opportunity for trial and error, experiences outside of Indian culture, and peer pressure. Children are expected to be home immediately after school. Even at home, down time is discouraged – homework and studying are overly emphasized.
- The Indian belief is that the first 25 years are to build character, education and empower oneself with achievements whether in spelling bees, tennis championships, or other activities. This belief that energy is limited and has to be channeled very strictly can cause a great deal of stress among children.
- Indian parents do not trust the western style of "hanging out," i.e. purposeless socializing on the street or in malls. It is seen as troublesome, risky, and a sheer waste of time. They do not see any social value in spending time without a specific purpose, i.e. education, information gathering, or achieving excellence. Sports, athletics, or social activities are viewed as distractions.
- Parents tend to dictate children's choices of education and their profession. They are insensitive to the individuality or personal choices of the child. Indians for the most part are thinking that the goal of education should be attaining both status and money. Their children may resent being coerced into becoming a doctor or a lawyer. They are essentially given prepackaged options.
- Children complain as to whom to trust about sharing their feelings. This ends up with suppressed or repressed feelings. Straight A's and academic success is used by parents to deduce that their children have no real emotional issues or needs.
- Children also express significant anxiety about sex-related issues.
- Typically, the children see their mothers as assertive and their fathers as somewhat effeminate.
- Most children in the camp expressed the need for attention, closeness, and recognition. Regardless of their future plans, they all felt they needed to be "the best," i.e. stand out academically and professionally.
- Indian girls have a hard time because they are "not being allowed to talk about boys at home." They manifest their anger by yelling at others in the family or by withdrawing.

- As they mature and enter adulthood, youths often feel resentful if they are expected to have an arranged marriage rather than merely for love. Although arranged marriages are fast disappearing in the Indian Diaspora, the practice reflects the traditional Hindu view that marriage is supposed to serve more of a social and family function than a strictly individual one. The core belief is responsibility first, love and sex later.

The Elderly

Indian family dynamics revolve around loyalty, hierarchy, dependence, and duty-over-feelings. Sacrificing individuality keeps the elderly in a purposeful role. Elderly men refocus more on spirituality, while elderly women take on managerial and mediating roles. Traditionally, the elderly have been known not to fear death, seek vanity, live in denial or exhibit any significant mental illness.

The role of the elderly in the Indian family dynamic is best understood in the context of the Hindu concept of the four phases of life, which will be discussed later in this book. In this worldview, the elderly male is in the Vanaprastha phase, and is expected to begin to disengage from the rat race, family entanglements, and intensify subordination of his energy into spiritual pursuits and serving the larger society.

Some other observations:

- It is an unspoken contract that the Indian elderly expect to depend on younger generation for their needs. The younger generation is obligated to pay their dues, prove their respect and loyalty to older family members.
- Sons, in particular the eldest, are expected to be the primary caretakers over and above their responsibilities as husbands and parents.
- Fortunately, Indian elderly live a rather minimalist life, sublimating their energies toward religious and spiritual practices. However their emotional neediness does not dissipate.
- The elderly exercise their hierarchical power as the conscience, super ego, and reminder of the moral duties of everyone to keep the family integrated, undivided and respected in the community.

Case Histories[1]

In this chapter, we will review some real-life case studies from my practice. The purpose is to introduce a few cases for orienting the community to the typical risks faced by the diaspora and to highlight that we are not immune to these situations.

The case studies involving children are discussed first, followed by those of adults.

Homicidal at Age Six

A 6-year-old Gujarati girl was referred to me because she attempted to drown her four-year-old brother in the tub. Her parents' elder brother, his wife, and two children had come from India to live with them. The parents were very loving and caring and lived in a two-bedroom apartment in New Jersey. The entire family was happy and well-adjusted until the great uncle's family came to live with them.

As culture dictates, the great uncle and his family were given priority. As a result, the girl lost her bedroom as well as her personal space. Not having a sympathetic ear to be heard, she resorted to protesting via hostile behavior. Once the parents were shown the dynamics and advised to stop alienating the girl, everything went back to normal.

Outstanding features of this case point out:

- Indians in India (IIN) are very comfortable with sharing space and sacrificing their personal comfort to accommodate relatives, seniors, and significant others. However, the same Indian child, if born or raised in the U.S., cannot conceptualize not having his or her own space.
- Indian children born or brought up in western cultures tend to have a very clear sense personal space, boundaries, individuality, and mutual privacy.
- Unlike in India, due to the context of extended family culture, the children brought up in western cultures tend to react to changes in their personal or family life as a traumatic experience.

---

[1] Names and identifying details have been changed to protect the privacy of individuals. Any resemblance to actual persons, or actual events is purely coincidental.

Unfocused Child

Anil was an 11 year old U.S. born fifth grader. His parents were Gujarat born immigrants living in Pennsylvania. They were concerned about his behavioral problems. He displayed an inability to accept structure and limitations, became easily excited, were very irritable, and lacked motivation. He was very demanding and demonstrated immature behavior. He displayed impulsivity and lacked focus. He was fearful of going to school and interacting with peers. The school's evaluation indicated an average IQ, friendly, talkative, student with symptoms of restlessness.

The family dynamics was complicated by Anil feeling that his father did not interact or help him with his homework. He saw his father as always being busy, and having too high expectations for his grades. His mother's cooking was very spicy which he did not like. Anil felt that nobody understood him.

Diagnostically he suffered from Attention Deficit Disorder and parent-child relational problems.

Outstanding features of the case point out:

- Family culture was conventional; expectations were high but without the acceptance of Anil's handicap and stress.
- Family did not positively reinforce his individuality.
- Father micro-managed – from his food preferences to his style of haircut.
- His exposure to mainstream society was limited to the interactions he had while at school.

Micromanaged Adolescent

Shyam is a 16 years old, younger of the two brothers, lives with his Bengal born, Hindu parents. Shyam's older brother also had emotional issues. He was prematurely born; kept for a few weeks in the hospital. He currently attends 11th grade. He has failed his driving license and still sleeps in his parents' bed. He has many hobbies, interests, and has no significant health issues. He is a very bright, tall and handsome adolescent with typical brown complexion and average Indian height.

Reasons for seeking psychotherapy were as follows:

- He threw a pencil and injured his mother's eye, has been kicking doors, procrastinates everything, appears depressed, unmotivated and avoids interaction with parents.
- He has numerous fears and phobias i.e. darkness, ghosts, heights, being alone and social anxiety. He feels scared to talk even though feels he has a lot to say. He has a severe stuttering problem.
- He has major sleeping problems, tosses and turns. When in his own room, he feels that his parents do not respect his space and constantly watch him to see what he is doing. He resents their constantly reminding him to study and stay off the computer. They want him to read actual books and not study via computer.
- He has been feeling increasingly isolated and anxious since 10th grade and feels preoccupied as to school/class and how peers do not respect him. He feels ugly, short, not respected and dumb.
- He feels great deal of stress involving his homework, anticipating academically failing and interacting with others, insecurity about not getting into a good college in the future.
- He holds grudges as to peers and parents and uses it to distance self from others.

Facts are that Shyam's parents are caring, good, simple, typical, and traditional. However, they feel comfortable only with the familiar as to how they grew up back home. As a result, the household culture is stagnant. It's not open for any new experience or interaction even if potentially positive. Any change is threatening to the parents and they expect the children in the household to stick to the familiar culture and routine. The mother and father always speak in one voice and lack any individuality. They are fearful of their son's sexual curiosities. They are obsessed that if their son does not study the traditional Indian ways, he may end up becoming ordinary or a failure. The parents managed all their anxieties and worries by hyper-focusing on their children rather than understanding their son's need for individuality and challenges of being an adolescent.

They avoid any and all focus on their parenting-related dysfunction. Shyam's parents obsess with the patient and have no hobbies or life of their own. Their social life revolves around their own provincial socials and functions. It also gives the parents a purpose and something to be preoccupied with in the absence of any personal ambitions, hobbies, or goals. They are self-absorbed. They dread the son's emotional needs and age appropriate curiosities. They behave as if they never left the middle-class neighborhood of Kolkata. Their core belief is that their son has a whole life for everything and now he should eat, sleep, and breathe only education. They fear new information, any introspection, and any therapeutic input for fear of being proven wrong and having to change.

Clinically, Shyam is suffering from Adolescent Adjustment disorder with depression and anxiety, multiple phobias and parent-child conflicts. But socially, emotionally and in terms of self-image he is basically stuck in a state of mind of a "child". He is fearful of growing up and moving into the adult word, which is exactly what his parents unwittingly have conveyed to him – that he is a child who needs to be micromanaged at least until he gets married and has his own children. Shyam had a physical disadvantage of being a "preemie" - delayed social skills, but the biggest complication has been parental rigidity, ignorance, fear of emotions, and closed mindedness to recognize Shyam as an individual. They have failed to facilitate his age appropriate autonomy. In essence, Shyam's symptoms were cries for help, need for attention and ambivalence about autonomy.

Recommendation in such cases, often, is "treat the parents and child will be cured". The dysfunctional parenting and failure to see the bigger picture based on realities of raising family abroad needs re-examination. For example, identifying boundaries that bedrooms are personal space unless something criminal, unhygienic, or dangerous is taking place.

Parents need to confront their own insecurities, irrational fears as immigrants, and control their over reactivity so not to convey to the child that he/she is damaged goods.

Confining and micromanaging the adolescent's socialization exclusively to own ethnic, provincial, community, and familiar situations works contrary to healthy adjustment in the school, acceptable peer interaction, as well as fitting in the neighborhood culture. The ideal approach should be "best of the both worlds".

In Indian culture, essentially the method of learning is based on role modelling/observational, while in the West it is based on a trial and error by the individual. Indian parenting follows an assembly line approach of raising clones unlike Western parenting which facilitates separation and individuality. In India, personal identity tends to be an extension of significant others, joint family, caste, community, traditions, culture, language, and religion. In the USA, individual identity is deliberately nurtured very early on.

Indian parents' need for control on the surface appears to be very loving but under the veneer it is fear of harm, unnecessary risk-taking, rebellious behavior, failure as to academic success and ultimately ending up an "Average Joe". These fears are so deeply and pervasively entrenched in the unconscious mind that they end up as obsessions and often jeopardize children's well-being.

Leave Me Alone

Vijai was an 18 year old college student, born in India and came to the US at age 6 months, lived with his parents and younger brother who had pervasive emotional handicaps. His father was a busy information technologist and his mother a housewife. Parents were not amenable to therapy for themselves in spite of major marital, parenting issues and their son's near-suicidal behavior. Vijai resisted therapy because he really wanted his parents to connect with him and avoid focus on self. He did not want to solve the problem by becoming mature and, instead, felt stuck in a "child" state of mind. He appeared underweight and malnourished.

Reasons for seeking therapy were as follows:

- Depression, episodic rage, "I do not care" attitude.
- History of panic attacks.
- Excessive sleeping and avoidance of any interacting with parents,
- He was angry with Indian female peers and Indians as a whole. He felt ashamed of being an Indian in the college and social settings.
- Had difficulty trusting people, in general, therapist and his parents. He anticipated "betrayal'? He felt his dad is clueless, self-absorbed, does not communicate and is overly demanding as to academic success and dictating as to what should be his major in the college. He saw his mother as obsessing with feeding him while he deprived himself of food.
- Preoccupied with feeling rejected by peers in school and particularly as to not having a girlfriend.
- Felt ugly, short, dark

Clinically, Vijai's protest that he does not care and wants to be left alone, is a mere façade. Underneath, he is crying for help, seeking attention, needing caring, nurturing, sharing and made to feel okay by his parents/ significant others.

Recommendations are clearly that he needs his parents to make a shift and reach out to him and learn to see him at a deeper level than just his superficial rage, alcohol abuse, avoidance drama and resisting to eat adequately. Everything about him is seeking parental attention and affection since unconsciously he knows his parents are psychologically "deaf, mute, dumb and fearful of change and personal responsibility". The family is existing by default since "no one is home" to allow feelings /emotions of each other to be nurtured.

Sharing is different from preaching, sermonizing and demanding. Becoming hyper-focused on studies is a turn off for younger people as they want to share about their fears, worries, social life and other issues.

Parenting gives the ultimate opportunity for parents to learn to play all over again and grow with the children. There is more to life than just highest qualification, familiar professionals and earning big money.

Traumatized Childhood

Preeti is a 23 year old, college educated, Hindu, U.S. born, and pretty female of slightly dark complexion. She resides with her south Indian parents and one younger sister and brother. She is unemployed. The family is quite dysfunctional because of the parents' marital crisis and financial hardship. Preeti has a significant history of Adult Attention Deficit Disorder with hyperactivity and chronic depression. Additionally, she has been abusing alcohol, bordering on dependency. She is very bright and aware of her parents' issues. She has tried to be independent. She has curiosity about Hindu religion, Indian culture and feels very compassionate about helping others.

Reasons for seeking psychotherapy were as follows:

- She grew up feeling that her parents were sarcastic, critical, and conveyed to her that she is incompetent and a failure. They discouraged and delayed her learning to drive and justified that an astrologer told them it will not be safe for her.
- She drank alcohol rather heavily for the previous 5 years while living in the dormitory and also had pervasive interpersonal fears, conflicts and always felt worthless. Preeti feels she does not belong anywhere and she is good for nothing.
- Her self-esteem is very low, mood depressed, and self-confidence impaired. She feels inadequate and incompetent. She was recently fired from her job and now she is in panic that no one will hire her. She worries a great deal as to her future.

Facts are that she was never properly diagnosed and assisted with her childhood disorder of being ADHD and depressive. Her parents were too busy with their marital issues and also making a living that they lacked awareness and interest as to what is happening to the children. They managed and coped by denying their children's emotional needs and concerns.

Clinically, she is suffering from depression, alcohol dependence, parent-child conflicts, and sibling conflicts. Preeti's need to be accepted by others is highly exaggerated and often results in rejections, adding to her depression, drinking, and self-put-downs. She is searching for a comfortable identity as well as autonomy as indicated by her pursuits to teach Indian philosophies, practice yoga, pilgrimage to Mount Kailash, and relinquish her ego.

Recommendations: Children are not born perfect and they have needs, have an individuality and may often have handicaps. Denials, ignorance, insensitivity or to escape in fantasy that all will magically get better is morbid parenting. Early diagnosis and intervention can avoid unnecessary suffering and confusion. Seeking professional help should be given a priority over the stigma and own insecurities. Child's wellbeing is more crucial than the fear of being seen as an imperfect family or having mental illness.

Preeti has lot of internal strengths i.e. goodness, ideals, drive to move forward, ambitions, intelligence, looks, etc. However, until and unless she learns about her personality and mastery as to her emotional overload triggering her dysfunctions she will continue to sabotage her happiness and independence.

Her psychotherapy focus should be to learn to cut the umbilical (psychological attachment) cord and work on finding and defining self, i.e. her own individuality.

People often come to therapy because of crisis like depression, alcoholism, and marriage problems but eventually end up focusing on "Who am I? How do I become a happier person? How do I manage my life without conflicts?"

Often alcoholism is a major challenge due to the addiction factor. But in this case it will disappear on its own once she is secure in her own "being or becoming" a competent adult. However, she will still have to refrain from drinking and learn to change people, places and things which evoke her pattern of drinking. Attending AA will definitely be an asset.

The Unhappy Wife

Ganga was a 23-year-old married woman with no children, who was born in Surat, and at age 20 came to the U.S. to join her husband. She lived in the U.S. with her husband, both in-laws, and a sister-in-law who was mentally handicapped. While cooking, cleaning, and taking care of the in-laws, she also held a job. Her husband was the only son, highly educated, a professional, and a strict vegetarian.

She came to see me because of episodes of depression with suicidal thoughts, pervasive dissatisfaction, crying, feeling fed up with her life, having difficulty functioning in the wife role, inability to sleep, and overreacting to even small irritations. She repeatedly injured herself by peeling her skin.

She was fearful of becoming pregnant because she did not want the child to be trapped. She had lost all interest in living. She did not want to live with her husband, but she did not want to abandon him either, as he was a very caring husband. He just could not establish boundaries between himself and his mother. She was regretful of ever having married in the first place.

Once she had even returned to India to distance herself from her in-laws. She described her mother-in-law as self-absorbed, never satisfied, super religious, unhappy with her own husband, and obsessing with her son in terms of all her expectations being met by him. Her world revolved around her son. She had many health problems and faked her dependence to the extreme.

The causes of – the absolutely unnecessary – suffering were the following: the mother-in-law did not want to accept the daughter-in-law or any change in the household culture, as required after her marriage. The more she felt dependent, the more she feared losing control over her son. Her concept of loyalty was morbid and she chose sadistic ways to exercise her control. The son was naïve about his mother's symbiotic relationship with him, and failed to renegotiate his husband role with his mother. He was unwilling to take on an adult and husband role due to cultural guilt and an unspoken oath of blind loyalty to his parents.

The Ivy League Graduate

Manohar was a 32-year-old single male and Ivy League graduate, employed in the hedge fund industry. He had Ph.D. in Financial Engineering. His father died when he was 22, and his mother lived in

India. His grandfather died at age 42 due to alcoholism. His mother was known to be chronically dissatisfied with her life because she had given up her education and ambitions due to marriage at age 18. The patient revealed that his childhood was full of embarrassment and difficulties because of father's alcoholism, power struggles between his father and grandfather, and marital arguments.

He consulted me for having impulsively resigned from his high paying job following an episode of extreme rage, acting out, confusion, paranoia, and delusional behavior toward his coworker. He had ended up in a psychiatric hospital.

Outstanding features of this case point out:

- He suffered from bipolar mood disorder which triggered a manic episode resulting in delusional behavior and impulsive resignation i.e. impaired judgment.
- He was neither properly diagnosed nor complying with the medication, counseling, required life style changes and practice of yoga for self-help, all of which are necessary for the treatment of bipolar mood disorder.
- His unresolved chronic childhood dependency issues rooted in his relationship conflicts with parents which were unmet in spite of his being 32 years old, and his academic and professional achievements.
- His brilliance and success provided him with intellectual cover but no resolution of his ambivalence toward his mother, fear of being on his own and of getting married

> *Childhood traumas, relation-ship conflicts, and psycho-social confusion tend to linger on indefinitely and result in emotional handicaps unless addressed in psychotherapy.*

and settling down. His fear was rooted in his childhood memories of his parents' miserable marriage.

The Breadwinner

Anita was a 32-year old, college educated, Brahman, conservative female married to a Lucknow, India-born Non-Resident Indian (NRI). The marriage took place during a brief visit of her husband to India. After the marriage, she stayed with her in-laws in the U.S. Her husband was extremely attached (symbiotic) to his father and behaved like a little boy. His elder sister was dictatorial and the decision maker.

Anita developed depression after six months of living with the joint family. Instead of the family respecting their privacy and autonomy, they did just the opposite. The husband and in-laws were violent and physically abusive to her including locking her out of the house. She had no family or friends in the U.S.

She was the breadwinner of the household. She became pregnant which only worsened the situation. Her husband was emotionally dependent on his family-of-origin while financially dependent on his wife. Following prolonged violence, she moved, to live on her own, with her infant daughter. Her husband joined her but spent most of his time with his father and sister. He was unable to hold a job, became depressed, and grew increasingly more dependent (clinging). He was not able to function in the role of a husband or a father due to his extreme dependent personality. In spite of being mistreated by her brother and sister-in-law during her childhood in India, she had no prior history of any emotional or interpersonal problems.

She came to see me because of severe depression, violent outbursts, loss of appetite, inability to function at work, insomnia, pervasive conflicts with her in-laws, and an inability to cope with her husband's personality dysfunction. She had acted out dangerously and destructively. She felt powerless and despondent but due to cultural factors was neither open to separation nor returning to India. She initially was against her husband seeking professional help or medication. She herself was not open to seeking help. The conflicts went on for many years, with prolonged suffering, mutual violence, and repeated involvement of the police and the legal institution. The last I saw, she was living alone with her daughter.

Outstanding features of this case point out:

- It was an arranged marriage, carried out on short notice, and matching was based on caste, class, and the husband being in the U.S. She had the expectation that the marriage would meet all her emotional needs. She would be at her best in running her household, and above all, would finally become free from the demands of her extended family.
- Her husband suffered from borderline personality disorder. His dependency was enabled and exploited by his parents and sister. The existence of mental problems was ignored.
- They never expected, encouraged, or promoted autonomy or mutually productive adult roles and instead enabled incompetence and infantile dependence. Above all, the entire family became

united under the pretense of feeling victimized. Their hostility towards Anita was unconscious and an exercise in controlling behavior.

- They were not open to feedback or professional help. They solved all their problems by blaming the victim and seeing their son as the ultimate victim. The husband's core conflict revolved around not being able to separate and adequately function in his roles as son, brother, husband, father, and ultimately as an adult in the community.

The patient was exhausted with an overload of responsibility, pervasive sabotage by her in-laws, having total financial responsibility of the household and an absolutely hopeless future. Her aggression was a survival mechanism representing her despondence, feeling trapped and rendered helpless.

Irony of Vengeance

This is about a young, successful, but very depressed Indian professional, whose spouse was also a successful professional. They had serious personality incompatibilities because of differences in their socio-economic backgrounds. He saw his wife as wasteful, immature and aggressive. She perceived him as cheap, thrifty, money obsessed with no regard for feelings and fun. They never sought professional help as they did not want to be exposed. The marriage ended abruptly when the wife killed herself and her only child, so that her husband could collect a large insurance settlement.

Outstanding features of this case point out:

- Marital power struggles were symbolic of their incompatibilities, class differences and lack of awareness and openness to seek professional help.
- Wife most likely had serious emotional problems and the marriage was the perfect stage to act out her childhood conflicts involving her parents, etc.
- Either of the spouses could have gone for individual counseling and broken the vicious cycle that lead to murder-suicide.
- Both spouses got hooked into the money obsession, forgetting that other powerful emotions were churning and also needed to be addressed.
- Feelings not dealt with tend to spill over either in terms of accident proneness, physical illness or outright mental illness.

- Passive-aggressive behavior tends to be destructive as it does not allow open communication, taking responsibility, and resolution. It harbors anger and hostility without allowing an opportunity for the other person to remedy it. Indians often resort to this pattern for fear of losing control, retaliation by others, harmful consequences, or loss of self-esteem. However, properly sublimated and constructively redirected it can prove to be useful. M. Gandhi defeated the British with this passive-aggressive maneuver. Without a doubt, in interpersonal transactions and relationships, it is much more constructive to be open, direct, and sincere in asserting one's thoughts and feelings. One gets in life what one negotiates for. If you communicate nothing, the chances are you will only end up feeling frustrated and dissatisfied. .

The Shoplifter

Prema was middle-aged, born and raised in India, the youngest of five siblings, and had her degree in microbiology. She came to the U.S. in 1984, got married in 1985 and had a daughter. When I saw her, she had been married for 19 years and was employed in the food and beverage industry. Her husband also had a college degree and an outstanding job.

She came to see me because she was being charged for repeated shoplifting offenses. She wanted help only to avoid jail, and had no interest in understanding or managing her shoplifting compulsion. She thought paying a fee for the services and the report was a waste. In addition, she wanted nobody else to be involved. As a result, it was next to impossible to even schedule appointments with her.

Her secretiveness, denial of reality (that she cannot manage her third offense without legal implications), resisting to pay for services, and difficulty in communicating on the phone, made it very difficult for me to help her. As she was non-compliant, I have no idea as to her fate.

Outstanding features of this case point out:

- Her biggest handicap was her inability to trust and relinquish control.
- She was in denial of the nature of her problem which had to do with impulse disorder, loss of control and ambivalence about attention seeking.
- She was also unconsciously punishing her husband by being passive aggressive.

- She had extreme obsessive preoccupation regarding money. She had no separate funds outside of her marital bank accounts.

Please Come to My Pity Party

Purnima is 40 years old, married for over 16 years, college educated, a mother of two adolescents, and resident in the USA for the past 15 years. Her parents live in India. She maintains almost daily contact with them and her siblings. She has a history of depression and childhood sexual trauma. She suffers from thyroid disorder. She drinks socially and loves Indian parties. She wants to work but has paralyzing fears of failure, being rejected and being seen as stupid. So she avoids being interviewed and even in social situations compulsively compares and concludes not being rich enough, successful enough or that she will ever amount to be anything.

Reasons for psychotherapy were as follows:

- Depression; feelings of worthlessness, inadequacy, self-doubts, low self-esteem and "doom-gloom". Self-perception as a total failure.
- Absence of pleasure in anything. Often complained "I feel blank".
- Pervasive anxiety, fears and episodic panic attacks.
- Nightmares, excessive intolerance of uncertainty.
- Confusion and concerns about future.
- Fears bordering on paranoia that others will reject her. Excessive focus/preoccupation on "others".
- Blamed self or her husband for her not being rich and successful, being moody, and not helping.
- Marital problems.
- Avoidance and sense of incompetence as to decision making.
- Intolerance of leisure time and inability to utilize it and filling it with worrying.
- Seeing everything as a problem and perpetually obsessing and fearing doom and gloom.

Facts revealed that Purnima grew up in a very authoritative household, particularly her father told her she was a failure, and she achieved low grades while in school. Her exposure as a child and adolescent was very limited as she had no outside exposure other than the family and school. She had no hobbies, friend circle or ever had the opportunity to interact with new and unfamiliar situations or people. She felt safe within the confines of her home, marriage and immediate social milieu. As a consequence of an overly protected and highly criticized upbringing, she never developed psychologically as an "adult", socially competent and with good self-image.

Clinically, Purnima suffered from depression, Generalized Anxiety Disorder, Obsessive Compulsive Disorder, parent-child problems and marital problems. In spite of intelligence and numerous other assets and resources, she often came across as intellectually borderline.

Recommendations required the following:

- Skills to process, label and verbalize her feelings to minimize confusion and emotional overload and emotional roller coaster. Encouraged to take risks by gradual exposure to the new situations such as shopping malls, gym, job interviews, etc.
- Management of cognitive overload by learning to think rationally, objectively and keeping things simple.
- Skills provided to stop personalizing everything, constantly comparing self with others and self-pity.
- Decision-making skills promoted by learning to separate issues, facts, subjectivity, learning to prioritize and separate reality from imagination.
- Instructed not to cling to her family of origin by daily phone calls and allowing **long distance input** by parents and siblings. She was also negatively reinforced from attending and constantly socializing via Indian parties since she always felt others bragging made her feel failure and reduced her time to socialize by mainstreaming herself. Remaining 24/7 in "Indian ghetto" stunts emotional growth and skills development and flourishing in the context of diverse culture and resources utilization available in the host country.
- Marital and family therapy was recommended to promote team approach, honest communication and conflict resolutions. In essence, to remove family unit dysfunctions to allow each person to be responsible.

The Conservative Brahmin

Triveni was an India-born 48-year-old female, married to a very conservative Indian whose family lived in London, UK. He was raised there. She consulted me initially for nervousness, excessive fears, and an inability to function in her roles as a wife and an adult. She was perpetually sad, ready to cry, and lacked any confidence and self-esteem. She was unable to enjoy anything and was extremely insecure. Her background included a history of family mental illness. She had undergone numerous psychiatric treatments as well as counseling, but with no improvement or any hope for anything ever to change.

She often reported anticipating failure, helplessness, confusion, and doom and gloom. The rare occasions she felt any reprieve was when her husband was away from home or when she travelled to India. She saw her husband as loud, bossy, aggressive, controlling, critical, and disapproving, and felt that she could never please him. She felt abandoned by her husband and blamed him for making her feel insecure and nervous. She had had three mental breakdowns prior to seeing me.

My interviews with the husband revealed that in spite of having lived in England and now in the USA, he was stuck in his conservative, Brahmanic ways and was excessively obsessive, and fixated on his wife. He participated in the mutual suffering as if that was the only game in town. He would force her to come for therapy but, at the same time, was never convinced that changes by him could improve the culture of his home or that he would benefit from it. No matter what suggestions were made, he was unable to let go of the past and often blamed her for not telling him before the marriage that she had a family history of mental problems. He really lacked any and all empathy for his wife and locked her in a role of being "dishonest, playing negative games, and being lazy." He never stopped comparing her with other women, or trying to prove her as incompetent.

Outstanding features of this case point out:

- Her distress was internal due to family history and her own mental illness, but her husband used her as a scapegoat due to his pent up rage and his need to avoid focus on self. This was a major factor in her repeated hospitalizations and chronic melancholia.
- Her husband needed counseling but was not open to it or willing. He preferred his wife to be the designated mental patient in the family. The husband's inability to live in "here and now," and unwillingness to relinquish his clinging to his family of origin, who lived in England, was a maneuver to avoid growing up and letting go of his bitterness.
- Wife had no resources or support system to be on her own and therefore there was no hope for the family/marriage system to change.

Emotional Beggar

Sneha is a 50 year old Hindu, female, Mumbai born and raised, college educated, married for 26 years, and lives with her husband and 19-year-old daughter. Prior to her marriage she was a successful model and well paid at her job. Before to coming to the US, they lived and owned a house in Australia. Her husband is a highly paid sales executive and travels a lot for work.

Her reasons for seeking psycho-therapy were as follows:

- Total loss of confidence, self-respect, self-esteem and pervasive helplessness.
- Crying, sadness, excessive anxiety as to finances, future and marriage.
- Overwhelmed with feeling reduced, insignificant, unloved, loss of purpose and direction.
- Frustrated with her husband's excluding her, drinking, leaving the house messy, demanding her to financially contribute in spite of knowing that she has no job nor work visa.
- She felt trapped as her husband did not engage in any communication or sharing in spite of her desperate efforts to write letters, invite him for therapy, etc.

The facts were that Sneha was totally invested exclusively in marriage and had avoided independent friendships, pursuing hobbies, or acquiring skills for future use. She had ignored any and all contingency planning and had no alternatives.

Her expectations, even though minimum, from her marriage were rooted in an illusion that her husband has empathy and cares. Her naiveté had blinded her from realizing that her husband was emotionally bankrupt, self-absorbed, and single track minded. In essence, he was absent in the husband role.

Clinically, she was suffering from depression because of marital problems.

Her helplessness was because of overwhelming feelings of fantasy based "paradise lost", trapped with nobody or place to turn to and an unrealistic need to be loved by significant others. Her fears, worries, anxiety, loneliness, isolation, and finally the realization of her dysfunctional marriage as well as mother-daughter relationship triggered the crisis. She felt emotionally despondent and paralyzed in spite of being brilliant, talented, and versatile.

Recommendations for Sneha were, essentially, to pursue a multidimensional strategy. She needed to buy time to equip herself to face the challenges, i.e. adequate money to sustain herself for six months, decide to return home or continue living abroad, and procuring employment.

In the meantime, she needed to reduce her dependency on her husband and clinging to her daughter by minimizing all non-essential interaction and verbal exchange. (I often tell my patients not to speak unless it involves blood, flood, fire, or a health emergency.) Speak only in a few words if possible. Such an approach is intended to create a constructive crisis to force sharing and, hopefully, resolution. However, the risk is inherent as it may lead to divorce, violence, or self-injury. However, the goal is to alter the significant other's perception of her as a clinger, whiny, needy, pathetic, attention seeking infant.

Letter writing was advised to convey the seriousness of the situation and to provide clarity to the significant others that her needs are very basic and she is willing to do her part to reduce the tension. Psychotherapists can be of major assistance in formulating a source of constructive letters to neutralize power struggles and destructive interactions.

She needed to take her psychotherapy sessions seriously, even when her husband and daughter refused to participate. She was advised to keep all clinical feedback very confidential to prevent emotional blackmail by significant others. Psychiatric consultation included advice to consider medication.

She needed to also avoid involving friends, relatives, and parents in her marital conflicts to prevent unproductive exposure and useless input. She was encouraged to attend the gym, pursue hobbies, and accumulate funds.

Psychologically speaking, prevention is better than cure. One gets in life what one negotiates for. Relationships require direct dialogue regarding values, beliefs, habits, preferences, priorities, expectations, strength and weaknesses. Verbalizations do not always guarantee accuracy and genuineness since one may not have the emotional maturity or the clarity as to one's personality makeup. Therefore, one should be vigilant as to behaviors and patterns occurring in different real life situations and changing context.

Emotions (anger, fear, jealousy, sadness, and happiness, etc.) play a powerful role in determining one's behavior. Often, culturally sensitive

Indians tend to downplay and deny emotions in order to be seen as in control and superior. One displaying excessive panic, worrying, and irrational anger needs to be avoided due to their emotional immaturity.

Like happiness, Emotional Intimacy is not natural to human beings even though everybody loves to profess it. Happiness requires resolution and determination to pursue it similar to intimacy which requires respect, responsibility, caring, and sharing with others. Trusting is a tough skill to acquire and manage.

Denials, delays, rationalizations, minimizing, and expecting magic to happen only guarantees the compounding of conflicts, distress, and alienation.

Gender, caste, regional, religious, provincial, subcultural differences are real but not surmountable and play important role in relationships. They need to be openly discussed, issues clarified, and resolved before any commitment is made to get married, migrate, raise children, etc.

It cannot be overemphasized that "Lovers tend to be blind." Chemistry of emotion cannot be trusted and therefore it is crucial to verbalize one's belief system and expectations. Needs and wants must be clearly expressed and every attempt should be made to ensure that the other person is capable and concentrating when such communications take place. The sooner one realizes that others cannot read your mind, the better the chances for healthier relationships.

If I Do Not Win, No One Wins

Shanti was a 52 year old, college educated, Delhi born, mother of two adolescent sons, divorced, living in the US. She had a long history of job dissatisfaction and highly conflicted relationships at work. She was either fired or dreaded and avoided. She has always been under employed in spite of her high IQ, excellent verbal skills and coming across as sophisticated. She was involved in extremely difficult post-divorce court battles over child support and other parenting issues – though not totally her fault. She was also extremely angry with her elderly parents, back home in India and resented her two older sisters over manipulating her parents and depriving her of her inheritance. She had chronic, serious and complex psychosomatic diseases since the beginning of her adulthood and had frequent flare ups with damaging consequences. She was totally consumed with feeling abandoned by her parents, manipulated by her sisters, victimized by her ex-husband and the court system for the past 9 years, and anticipation of not being appreciated by her two sons for all her sacrifices. Her work related distress was always present. She actively sustained her conflicts and, as a result, felt abandoned and helpless.

Reasons for psychotherapy were as follows:

- Psychosomatic disorder and flare ups causing Gastro-intestinal, rectal and sexual dysfunction.
- Bouts of depression. Sense of failure, loss of direction, loneliness
- Ongoing anxiety, frequent panic attacks and overwhelming worries that she will not be able to sustain herself financially, etc.
- Excessive and paralyzing ambivalence whether to live here or in India, sustain court battles or let go, clinging or distancing from her sons, parents, sisters, holding on to the past or being in the moment, etc.

Facts are that Shanti is divorced, parents have their own life and independent minds, and sisters are local in India so have an advantage over her as to controlling things locally and that court system does not offer any guarantee for justice or making her husband accountable. It should also be realized that no matter how much sacrifice she makes as a parent, it's not constructive to manipulate children to feel good or to make them a middleman in dealing with her parents. Facts are she is very resourceful and her own assets are good enough to produce financial security, peace of mind and even professional success.

Clinically she was suffering from Post-Traumatic Stress Disorder, acute/chronic stress, depression, anxiety and panic disorder, psychosomatic disorder, parent-child conflict. Possibility of Dependent Personality was noticeable even though she, on the surface, appeared a successful adult.

Recommendations are that she should primarily understand her "addiction" to rage and feelings of helplessness. These chronic feelings are destroying her body but also all relationships and adequate utilization of her intellect, education, leadership, and many more assets and resources she has. If it's not her abdomen, rectum or vagina then it's her orality which fuels aggression.

She should stop receiving and calling her parents and siblings and allow some distance, detachment and cooling off period. Phone calls are symbolic of the umbilical cord not being cut in spite of her being 52 years old. Court battle with former husband, too, symbolize failure to sever umbilical cord. Excessive concern as to how children will relate to her is also indicative of her "umbilical cord" now attached to the kids.

Deliberate practice and pursuit of relaxation, peace, happiness, humor, autonomy, "letting go" will be of immense benefit to neutralize power struggles, blaming and inflicting pain to significant others. In life, nobody really owes anything to anybody whether its love, loyalty, favors or security. It's wonderful if they happen. This realization will facilitate her independence from significant others. There is no substitute for "growing up" i.e. taking a bold plunge to face the adult world and consequences of one's own karmas. There is no one to hide behind and no place to run. Face it!

She needs conceptual clarity that the goal of interpersonal life has to be play "I win-you win" game and not "lose–lose" Mahabharata. The best way to change others is to change oneself and watch the magic happen.

She will continue to require anti-anxiety and anti-depression medication, periodic emergency room visits along with long term psychotherapy. She has significant assets and resources to improve in time.

No Place to Turn to

Ishwar is a 53 year old, India born, married for 24 years, college educated, and information technology professional who lives with his wife, two daughters and a son. He has been in the USA for the past 20 plus years. He has avoided seeing a psychologist due to the stigma in spite of the realization that he is overwhelmed, depressed, trapped in a vicious cycle and feels lost in his husband, father and provider roles. He is a very soft spoken, kind man who is very respectful to others. He has rather a dark complexion and does not put too much effort in making impressions.

His reasons for seeking psychotherapy were as follows:

- Feeling isolated, alienated, angry, confused and a failure but having no place or person to unload his feelings.
- He had lost all sense of pleasure (anhedonia) and also developed headaches.
- He felt put down and targeted by his both daughters but more so by his wife.
- He felt that he was breaking down and that his head will explode with the excessive and unreasonable dependency by his wife and children.

- He felt he has lost himself due to accommodating and trying to please significant others.
- Marital problems; shouting, blaming by wife and her failure to manage her own fears, insecurities, frustrations were becoming impossible for him to deal with.

Facts were that his marriage and family were stuck in "infantile mode" and they were all phobic of growing up and facing the outside world. In particular, his wife's clinging and yet blaming him was obviously calculated and rooted in her avoiding confronting her own "demons" of dependency. She was child in the grown up body of a woman.

He did not understand the intensity, complexity, interplay and the emotional "Mahabharata" at the core of his family and tried to survive it instead of confronting or seeking professional help.

His children were all dysfunctional and symptomatic of parental and their marital dysfunction and, above all, fearing that if any change was to be introduced then the system would collapse.

Clinically, Ishwar was depressed, suffered from chronic stress, marital and parent-child problems. His symptoms were indicative of his desperation, despondence and having no place to turn to. The cognitive and emotional overload was unbearable. He felt very enraged but helpless. He took total responsibility upon himself.

Obviously he did the right thing when sought professional help. It prevented the crisis. Before he could regain his composure and see things clearly, he needed to vent, unload and prevent mental breakdown or violent behavior.

Learning about stress management, whether through psychological techniques or additionally via detachment and distancing, vacationing, pilgrimage, was a prerequisite before he could lead the family or resume his provider role.

When people are vulnerable due to stress or conflict, the risk of alcohol/drug abuse, violent behavior, suicide or mental breakdown escalates and addressing them becomes a priority over stigma, magical thinking or doing thing.

Dependency issues of significant others are pervasive among Indian families (nuclear or extended, in India or as an immigrant) and become the primary source of conflicts, stress, crisis, marital conflicts, parent-child issues and financial exploitation. There are reported cases when

Indians have killed/shot/ poisoned significant others (parents, in laws, spouses and even children), and then committed suicide.

Full Time Martyr

Jasoda was 55 years old, twice married, psychiatrist by profession, India born living in the US with her elderly retired-from-army father. Her mother had died a few years previously while she was on her way to India, in the plane. Jasoda had no children but was very bonded with her extended family of origin, uncles and cousins, etc. She was a caring doctor and very nurturing in every other role including friends. She had no history of family mental illness or personal history of alcoholism. However, she had complex and serious health issues involving mainly the heart, to the extent that she had to go on disability. She was a model daughter, sister, cousin, Indian, American, friend but had no personal life since she always put herself into a caregiving roles – from family to stranger. She was incapable of hurting anybody's feelings.

Reasons for seeking psychotherapy were as follows:

- Pervasive feelings of depression and chronic stress.
- She felt stagnant all her life and was indecisive in pervasive ways.
- She had become addicted to gambling for a few years.
- She felt infantile in facing others/elders, significant members of the family and coped by becoming submissive, subservient allowing herself to be used her entire life. She saw herself as an ornament, actress and a puppet. She surrounded herself with needy people and felt close to none. She believed that she could not trust anyone in her moments of need in spite of life long sacrifices.
- At times she felt rage but was never able to address it or confront the issues or the people. Even at work, she felt a misfit and less than adequate.
- She felt handicapped to enjoy life, be solo, experiment with new things, and allow sensual/sexual feelings. In essence be herself.
- Facts were numerous to spell out her dynamics. She was brought up feeling special, sheltered and molded to be a perfect "child" and a daughter. Her first known trauma came when her husband abandoned her without an explanation, leaving her traumatized and too confused to further pursue her adult role. She gave up on her needs and emotions and silently vowed never ever to take a risk, feel emotionally needy or safe with others. Her repressed and suppressed anger immobilized her and cemented her fate.

- She continues to shuttle between India and America, remains single and carrying the burden left over from the past by others.

Clinically, Jasoda suffered from depression, Post-Traumatic Stress disorder and parent-child problems. She was punishing herself and all significant others by playing martyr and coping with life by becoming subservient and care taker as it protected her from being ever abandoned again. Until her father's death, she allowed him to be a parasite and also her second husband who was a psychopath and used her. They both left her riddled with responsibilities lasting her life time. Her failure to become an adult in spite of her high IQ, extreme sophistication, caring, kindness, etc. explains her unresolved dependency issues and need for "safety" at any cost.

Facts were complicated as her first traditional marriage was annulled. She was married to a NRI who abandoned her even before the honeymoon. She came to the US looking for him and found that he was already married and living with someone else. He refused any communication or assistance to her. It was an arranged marriage.

She ended up being helped, sheltered and coached to work via an old family acquaintance.

She always felt guilty for settling in the USA due to her patriotic feelings and eventually she returned to India.

Recommendations for her require ongoing psychotherapy not only for her dependency issues, compulsion to care and nurture others, but also to develop a suitable life style to protect her cardiac health. Learning to be assertive, negotiating relationships based on give and take, recognizing those who are emotional or financial parasites and protecting self from being used are indicated. She needs to learn risk-taking and explore the "wider world" instead of 24/7 living around primary family i.e. blood relatives.

I am Perfect, They All Are Crazy

Subodh was a 60 year old, married for 40 years, India born, male who shared house with his wife but lived totally alienated for years. He had two children and his relationship with them was also bitter. He immigrated to the US some 15 years previously. He had low earning jobs lasting short durations in spite of being a professional and college educated. They had no savings and his wife was the only one supporting them as well as paying mortgage.

He was in physically good shape and there was no history of any substance abuse i.e. alcoholism. His wife suffered from depression, post trauma stress disorder - her husband's personality problems were major contributory factors. One of the sons had also serious emotional handicaps and it was suspected that father's side of the family may have history of schizophrenia, paranoid type.

Reasons for therapy were as follows:

- His wife had decided, after 40 years of trying to survive his strange and paranoid behaviors, to give him one last chance to consult a psychologist to save the marriage. He did not come voluntarily in therapy, as is often the case.
- He blamed his wife for turning his kids against him, expecting too much from him, bad mouthing him, her taking over the household when he lost his job and that her side of the family had not helped financially. He took pride in his special heritage and explained his reason for marriage as rescuing his wife since his in-laws were experiencing hardship.
- He was angry with the whole world, except his guru, for not being there for him and socially and financially supporting him.
- He reported experiencing a great deal of stress at his work and that it has been always the case. He had a very choppy history of work, with regards to earnings as well as being liked.
- He was angry and would have episodes of anger lasting weeks.

Facts included that, from the very beginning of the marriage, he avoided and failed his wife, his father role, and as a provider. He usually spent months staying with and devotedly following a specific swami (religious guru). He had left her more than once for years when his whereabouts were not known to the family.

In reality his wife worked hard and paid household expenses and raised the family.

Clinically, Subodh suffered from depression, intermittent explosive disorder, marital problems, parent-child problems and Paranoid Personality Disorder.

His self-esteem was very low and he was chronically angry and depressed. However, he avoided introspection as well as feedback and thus showed a pattern of existing via blaming others for not taking care of him. His devotion to his guru had two implications; i.e. infantile dependence and very likely unrecognized homosexual inclinations. He threatened to sue the therapist and complained to authorities, instead of allowing help and conflict resolution. He believed that offense is the best defense approach and sabotaging any hope ever for things to become positive and constructive. Subodh showed a pattern of managing to survive on the periphery of life only, because his wife assumed the "adult role", otherwise he would either have been on welfare or in mental institution. The cultural solution of retreating into an ashram, going into Sanyasa offers an acceptable form of sublimation. However, it can be anticipated that he will do neither and instead will continue to live miserably and manipulate all significant others to join him.

Recommendations should be to support his wife in choosing divorce and getting on with her life since he was basically hopeless due to excessive paranoia, explosive anger, lack of insight and failure to take any personal responsibility and, above all, refusing to engage in counseling or consider medication. Children should also be supported to not feel guilty or responsible for their dad's difficulties and to find their own happiness. The dysfunction is so severe that it will only jeopardize children's sanity and their own family life.

In general, marriages – "love or arranged" – have equal chances of failure and becoming unhappy since they do not allow the context for both parties to be honest, real, factual, and practical; and to develop contractual understanding. Lovers tend to be "blind" psychologically and therefore put their best forward to make an impression and in the process never check out the person's values, beliefs, concepts, definitions, goals, and skills to manage negative feelings (anger, fear, jealousy, anxiety, etc.). Arranged marriages are even more risky since neither of the parties have any opportunity to compare notes, expectations, belief system and negotiate what their needs and limitations are.

Retired and Aimless

Vijay was a 70 year-old, Bombay-born Maharastrian who was married and had four sons. He was financially very successful, had retired from his job, and was continuing his real estate investments. He had no support system other than an extended in-law family. He was compelled to undergo counseling by his wife who was unable to tolerate his drinking habits. His children were unable to relate to him and felt resentment. His life revolved around his real estate, wife, and children.

Diagnostically he was depressed, had marital problems, parent-child issues, as well as alcohol dependence.

Outstanding features of this case point out:

- Vijay was a very kind individual, but was unable to cope with changes in routine and a new phase of life.
- He lived for his family, without a life of his own, and when his family achieved independence, he was lost.
- The more he tried to cling to the family, the more rejected he felt. He used alcohol to cope with his "pity party" and abandonment issues.
- He had no insight into his emotional neediness and its negative impact on significant others.
- He rationalized his drinking by blaming his wife, preferring her mother and brother over him.

Crowded but Lonely

Sonpal was an 85-year-old retired widower, who came to the U.S.A. to be with his three sons and grandchildren. When he arrived, only one of his children hosted him while his other sons refused to even communicate. He suffered severe depression, health problems, and was unable to overcome the humiliation and abandonment he felt by his two sons.

Diagnostically he suffered from major depression, phase of life problems, and parent-child problems.

Outstanding features of this case point out:

- Traditional expectation of extended family being united and displaying respect to him was the primary cause of his depression.
- Intergenerational conflicts among his significant others were pervasive. Additionally there was no willingness or openness to confront the issues. As a result he felt even more neglected, alienated, and pitiful.
- Immigration was intended to unite the family but it turned out to be painful, with the awareness that all his children and their families are not close to each other. Immigration is not a guarantee for a family to be happy ever after.

- Families need to negotiate openly about arrangements and expectations, whenever relatives or guests come to live with them or even visit temporarily.

Stages of Life: Foundation for Self-Help

Later in this book, we will discuss Self-help solutions for psychological issues the Indian diaspora has been facing. Before we discuss those solutions, it is useful to understand how humans develop over time. With a model of human development, we can anticipate, prepare, and have a sense of where the individual fits in the world, what meaning she can give to life, or where she is on the map of life.

One of the more appealing western models was developed by American psychologist Eric Erikson, who postulated that humans undergo eight stages of development. Erickson believed that people experience conflicts that serve as turning points for each. These conflicts are centered on either developing or failing to develop a particular psychological quality.

For example, the sixth stage of psychosocial development occurs during early adulthood and is characterized by reconciling issues of intimacy versus isolation. According to Erickson's theory, people who were successful during this stage were able to develop intimate and committed relationships. Those who were not successful were more likely to suffer emotional isolation, loneliness, and depression.

Although Erickson's theory holds merit, I favor another approach which is embedded in Hindu culture. This approach is rooted in Hindu Ashram concepts, which incorporate psycho-somato-socio-spiritualistic holism. This is the four Ashramas of Hinduism, which offer prescriptions for each phase of life from birth until 100. These ashramas lay out a comprehensive prescription for somato-psycho-socio-spiritual needs throughout the stages of life. As a result, one should never feel lost or lack a purpose in life. Ashramas are useful for psychotherapy and mental hygiene prescriptions.

The first phase of life, which ranges from age twelve to twenty five, is Brahmacharya. This phase emphasizes celibacy, perfecting physical health, developing moral character, learning to respect others, sacrificing personal pleasures, and prioritizing being a student and acquiring wisdom. Unlike in the West, the young are required to sublimate their sexuality, hedonism, and materialism in favor of cultivating character and relinquishing ego. This approach prevents unnecessary distractions and destructive experimentation and short-circuits the compulsion to prematurely declare manhood or womanhood. The senses are harnessed for the higher cause of preparing for the next phase of the rest of one's life.

Learning, in the Hindu tradition, is not just gathering information to become pseudo-independent, get a job, or obtain economic prosperity. It is not just about learning how to drive a car, rent an apartment, or manage finances. Instead, it is about the pursuit of wisdom. Pleasure, comfort, distraction, and sexuality are prohibited and sublimated. Instead, one learns the art and skills of self-management. Learning to convert raw energy, impulses, and desires into socially constructive outlets cannot be deferred until the adulthood and also cannot be suddenly integrated during the elderly years. Successful sublimation is a lifelong process; the earlier one starts the greater the promise of mastery.

For child development, this implies not pressuring the child to prematurely rush into growing up. She is to remain in "child mode" for an extended period, and surrender ego to the hierarchy of elders, family, and community. Cleverness, manipulation, self-centeredness, selfishness, arrogance, argumentativeness, defiance, indulgence through negatives behaviors like sex, drugs, and cigarettes are taboo. This is the blueprint the child, adolescent, and young adult is expected to follow for his first twenty-five years. He is not allowed to be a capitalist (motivated by money or buying power), a consumer, or a materialistic being.

The second phase, Grahastha, covers the period of the next 25 years, until age 50. This is the ideal case, but the actual time period depends on life circumstances. For example, if the family has no breadwinner, then it is incumbent upon the young to sacrifice education and be the wage earner. Or he might in other circumstances marry at a younger age for family reasons. Respect, obedience, responsibility, and sacrifice are among the essential ingredients of Hindu vocabulary.

Grahastha Ashrama recognizes humans' biological, psychological, and social needs. That includes engaging in sexual pleasure in marriage, procreation, practicing one's profession, and earning and accumulating wealth. It also recognizes that elders and parents must be cared and provided for at the same time one provides for one's own children. In Hindu culture, it is thus rather common that three generations live together as an extended or joint family. (This often includes siblings and their families.) The Hindu family operates like a clan and a battalion where every member has a defined place, role, duty, and status.

The family is like an axel of the larger society. Its role is not limited to bearing, rearing, but to provide modeling so they learn to conform, carries out their duties before claiming any separation-individuation i.e. living for self. Householder stage is viewed as the most crucial and central phase in Hindu tradition. Grahastha Ashram therefore presents the greatest challenges. It tests an individual's endurance, resilience, and preparedness. Fortunately, the proverb, "It takes a village to raise a child," is a living proof in Hindu society. The resources, responsibilities, discipline, modeling, and crises management are all shared.

Grahastha Ashram, in spite of engagement in sexual pleasures, materialistic entanglements and permission to experience hedonism, leaves one aspiring and fantasizing for a change. One waits for a break until the appropriate age and time wherein one has fulfilled his or her moral, social, familial, and professional obligations. Twenty-five years may not be long enough to meet all the expected challenges and, therefore, Grahastha may need to be extended. In Grahastha, it is imperative that one has resolved, if not totally fulfilled, one's biological and sexual needs.

The next phase of Vanaprastha brings back the need to revive sublimation. One cannot begin unless one is ready to take the sublimation to a higher level of transcendence: the pursuit of serving (Sewa) the larger society and spirituality. The risk of becoming corrupt, deviant, or sociopathic is much higher if one has not gone through the nitty-gritty experiences of the Grahastha phase. Here, sublimation demands absolute self-discipline of thought, feelings, and motivational

It's paradoxical that decision making is influenced by emotions and vice versa. Ideally it should be based on the ability to integrate the maximum possible variables one can imagine. In reality decisions are based on stress, threats, demands, compulsions, desires, impulses, duty, needs, and wants. The most important considerations in decision making one has to take are independence from others and balancing conflicting demands, hopefully with a clear understanding of the larger context. Hindu personality tends to struggle between duty, others' expectations, and at the cost of self, autonomy, and feelings. If decision making feels overwhelming or ambivalence dominates the choices, then it's time to seek psychological counseling. A proactive approach has the potential to minimize damage and emotional suffering. To learn, improve, or make better decisions is one of the reason individuals consult mental health professionals.

objectivity, emotional neutrality, and maximum simplicity of action. The process of sublimation can be defined as converting raw energy, (aggression, sexuality, fear, instincts, and impulses) into refined thoughts, feelings and actions which will nurture, support, and benefit the larger society. Every aspect of Hindu Dharma is geared toward this single goal from birth to Moksha (liberation from the cycle of death and rebirth).

Vanaprastha Ashram covers the period of 25 years ranging from ages 51 to 76. In Sanskrit, Vanaprastha literally means departure for the jungle or retiring to the forest. "Jungle" is a metaphor for taking inventory of personal dharma, solitude, detachment, disengagement and relinquishing "I", "me" and "mine." When one is ready to let go of one's ego, one can truly become free even before death. From birth, a Hindu is expected to realize this and work hard during every phase of life to relinquish it. Ego is viewed as the source of ignorance, and ignorance is considered the source of all suffering. Ego is inseparable from capitalism, as it has become the trademark of individuality in the West. To retain or embrace ego and to operate from it, in the perspective of Hindu psychology, is sheer masochism and spiritual suicide.

The Vanaprastha phase, in a superficial way, is similar to retirement in the West. Unlike retirement in the capitalistic society, the Vanaprastha person does not seek engagement or spend his lifelong acquired wisdom in playing golf or bingo, filling time with hobbies, babysitting, or returning to part-time earning.

The final phase is Sannyasa, or renounced life. This last stage extends until death (ideally to age 100), with the focus being on total resignation, detachment from family, society, money, sex, and desires. This is accomplished by giving up one's birth name, religion and all possessions. By relinquishing one's familiar psychological identity, one can then leisurely and fully devote one's energy in either pursuing Nirvana or social service without any ulterior motives.

Sankhya-Yoga school is one the seven systems of Indian psychology, the goal, in essence, being internal and interpersonal harmony and creating a context for the realization of one's total potential. Sankhya is the theory of yoga, while yoga is the practice of Sankhya. It consists of eight steps: Yama, Niyama, Asana, Pranayama, Prityahara, Dharna, Dhayan, and Samadhi.

Yama to Dhayan have direct relevance to managing mind, body, and behavior. They're relevant to not only preventing physical or emotional distress but also facilitating happiness. The last step of Samadhi has religious-spiritual implications as it is expected to lead to Moksha or freedom from the cycle of birth and death. Regular practice of Sankhya Yoga is powerful tool for self-help, not only during Vanaprastha but through all stages of life. Variants of this practice are becoming mainstream all over the world, and are being utilized by organizations that include governments, corporations and the military.

Brahmacharya: Challenges and Solutions

Childhood still tends to be rather simple, innocent and well understood by and among Indians. It does not threaten parents as often the children tend to be cooperative, compliant and controlled. However, adolescence in the context of Indian Diaspora living abroad becomes a major challenge. Adolescents need their personal space, permission to carry out trial and error, and acquire skills to negotiate cross cultural interactions. This is also the time, to learn to bond with peers of all races, religions and cultures. Indian children and parents have the toughest time to amiably and constructively resolve the challenges faced by adolescents. Risk of power struggle increases unless handled by the parents with empathy, tolerance and by renegotiating new boundaries. Adolescents seek personal identity and crave for unique individuality and it is often mistaken for rebellion and setting self up for life long failure. The doom gloom is unnecessary since it's a natural evolution and response to meet the challenges of school, peers, sustaining self-esteem and reprocessing one's family with different pigmentation and culture. If properly supported and managed, adolescents return to their roots but only after a period of defining themselves. In some cases this phase may last 20 years.

Case of a Hybrid Kid

Avinash was a 24 year-old, eldest of two, male born in the USA. His parents got married in India after his mother accepted Hinduism. His Father was from brahamin background while mother was born in Cuba and brought up in the USA. Both parents were very successful professionals but went through usual marital challenges due to differences in values and priorities.

Avinash suffered from health issues early on and later was picked on by peers and bullied a great deal. As a result he had to change schools. During his adolescence, he felt embarrassed of his parents, home culture and felt he did not fit anywhere. Academically, he did well but socially he felt inadequate, awkward, vulnerable and maladjusted. Often he felt depressed and even contemplated suicide. He felt overwhelmed. In his desperate attempts to cope, he changed his name to a very common Christian name and even went through a few years of Christianization. Eventually, he underwent psychotherapy and it took years but felt improved self-image, freedom from seeking others' approval and overwhelming feelings of inadequacy.

Clinically, early illness of the childhood made him predisposed to feeling vulnerable. Parents being of different cultures and background added to his confusion. Early on when he needed to feel separate and perfect his own individuality, he lacked confidence and as a result, failed to acquire necessary skills to be independent and assertive. Single most important factor of his excessive need to be accepted, approved by others sabotaged his own intelligence, and other abundant positive qualities. It took him longer than his peers to establish successfully in terms of finances and professionally. Diagnostically, his major issue was dependent personality and depressive disorder.

Recommendations are that his parents should have gone through individual and marital psychotherapy before deciding to have children, resolved their differences of parenting style and removed the stress from the marriage. Avinash underwent serious counseling and that protected him from possible suicide and mental breakdown. Parents and Avinash both needed to take a long term view and work together on project independence and working together as a team.

Following are some of the general recommendations that parents should be cognizant and open to incorporate in dealing with their children through Brahmacharya phase

Problems are often not easily verbalized or conveyed. Therefore it's important to not rely totally on verbal interaction but to pay careful attention to any and all behavioral changes in the child such as insomnia, irritability, decline in school performance, impaired appetite, etc.

It is wise not to be overly hyper focused on academic achievements alone. It's crucial that children's feelings are observed and addressed. Excessive denial or intellectual approach can be lethal.

All children worry about their parents and their wellbeing. They often have fears that parents will die and what will happen to them. It's wise to listen and reassure them. Children usually have a highly developed intuition to "read parents emotions". Lying and denial will only worry them more. It's important to share with them in balanced manner.

Children or the country should not be criticized for loving the country in which they are born. Their association with India, Indians, Indian culture, and Indian religion are weaker and only marginal in spite of community exposure. Allow them to grow into it without demanding.

- Drug use is lot more common among adolescents than generally realized. Indians are not immune to it. Taboos should be openly talked about and expectations should be clearly verbalized that it's not our family and cultural tradition to do drugs, have babies before or outside marriage or to engage in breaking the law, The zero tolerance should be communicated in the context of what ideal Indian values are. .Often this will provide structure and guide the adolescent in tempting times. In the event, taboos are broken, it's very important to not abandon the child/adolescent and instead proper treatment should be pursued.

- For the child, separations, divorces, relocations, abrupt changes, marital conflicts, domestic violence, financial insecurities, and obsessing with money or material things can be significant causes of stress and contempt toward parents.

- Mood disorders like depressions and bipolar disorder are starting to appear much earlier among children. Mood disorders may appear as problems at school or sudden defiance or violence. They also may be brought on by drug or alcohol use. Early action and intervention is advised.

- Be attentive to children's conduct-related problems, oppositional behavior, personality changes, explosive episodes, class disruptive behavior, obsessive, compulsive, and ritualistic behavior as warning signs and do not ignore or minimize them.

- Children feel stress regardless how well they are provided, cared for or protected. Stress should be addressed. It can be lowered or alleviated by adjusting parental expectations, evaluating choices, and establishing a consistent routine and structure. It is often harmful to enroll a child in too many activities. "Keep it simple, stupid," as they say in Alcohol Anonymous.

- Parents should discourage materialistic values, minimize exposure to violence or unnecessary sexuality. Parents can encourage their child in utilizing healthy sublimations such as promoting interest in the larger world. This can be done through encouraging the learning of a foreign language, or helping develop an interest in other cultures. Instead of taking children instinctively to fast food restaurants, take them instead to ethnic restaurants, neighborhoods and markets. Let them see the bigger picture than just obsessing with grades, opposite sex or getting ready to make money in future.

- Parents should live life and should not make children the center of their universe. . Kids do not need to be made princes and princesses, told every five minutes that they are loved, that they are good, and can become anything they want to be. The reality is they have to learn to share space and things, make sacrifices, practice living by the family schedule, and enjoy life' simple joys and bonding with the family.

- Children are allergic to religion. Do not shove it down their throats. In time, they will return to their roots. There are other ways that you can utilize to make sure your kids are good human beings such as introducing more collectivism and less individualism, education and not materialism, giving and not taking, contentment, and not asking them to make a list of every gadget they wish to buy.

The schooling phase has become unusually stressful for children, families, and teachers. Parents have become neurotic not only due to the pressure of working, but because of self-doubts about their parenting skills. They fear that they have caused or will cause damage to their kids. They also fear that they will never turn out to be good enough parents, or anticipate that their kids will have low self-esteem, will not be well rounded, or end up using drugs. Teachers are overwhelmed because they are not allowed to be teachers but are expected to act as self-esteem builders, baby sitters, diagnosticians, therapists, and peacemakers. Everybody is sandwiched and overwhelmed and in the final analysis, children lose.

Each child is uniquely individual and has different limitations, resources and, in essence, unique personalities. Unlike robots, they follow their own pace, speed and creativity. Some are gifted, others are challenged, and rest fall in-between. They can also be handicapped, troubled, or just outright emotionally impaired. Parental openness, readiness, and empathy become vital, as is the need to seek interdisciplinary evaluations, procure adequate help, and adjust expectations. Parents need not act as adversaries to the school, specialists, and mental health professionals. It never hurts to seek many opinions, ask questions, and persevere until questions are answered, solutions or limitations are identified, and necessary resources are found. If parents feel ambivalent, or overwhelmed during the process, they then must seek out counseling for themselves.

Helping/treatment options and systems are rapidly evolving. Professionals are becoming more refined and the research is leading towards new solutions almost yearly. Therefore, the parental approach has to be one of working as a team and relinquishing unnecessary paranoia, fear, and intensity. They can start the process by self-help reading, Internet research, talking to the child's pediatrician, teacher, and counselor or calling their state or national psychology associations.

Students with special needs may need to see a school psychologist, social worker, learning consultant, audiologist, speech therapist, an internist, neurologist, ophthalmologist and/or a psychiatrist. Comprehensive evaluations are essential to finding the right solutions. Parents can initiate such requests.

There are several signs that indicate the need for early evaluations. Warning signs include sudden onset of impulsivity, hyperactivity, impaired attention, acting violently or self-destructively, behaving in a detached and self-preoccupied manner, and falling behind peers in school. Additional early indicators are a child's inability to organize and follow age-appropriate instructions, inability to understand what parents and the teacher are saying, forgetfulness, insomnia, nightmares, sleep walking, sudden defiance, stealing, and the inability to care for self.

Do not delay or waste time thinking he will outgrow these behaviors, or worry about social stigma and that the child will be labeled, or that you will face embarrassment. It's not about you but your child's long-term future. The best place to start is to make a file. Start observing and noting problem behaviors. Before seeing a professional, make sure you bring comprehensive information, including the mother's health during pregnancy, delivery, developmental milestones, history of diseases, hospitalization, injuries, medicines, and a list and addresses of other doctors.

Every time you see a professional, retain their business card and a copy of their reports in the file. Good records make it easier for a professional to see the bigger picture. Be sure to let the professional know if there are marital conflicts, spousal abuse, alcohol addiction, or any change in the family situation such as relocations or deaths. While waiting to see a professional, try hard to make sure the child is not doing drugs, being abused or traumatized, and that he is not experiencing sight, hearing, or speech impairments, or using medications which may be causing sluggishness or lethargy.

Vanaprastha: An Alternative to Western Retirement

The western motto of living is to be productive. As a result, work/ job and what one does for living becomes a central theme of one's life. For Indians work is what you do and it is not the essence of one's life. For example, most Indian parents do not encourage their children to work or earn while studying. In their minds, being a student is "all or nothing". They see earning/working as an obstruction and, at the very least, a distraction. Similarly, during Marital/householder phase Hindus see working, earning, providing and raising a family, etc. as essential priorities. The Vanaprastha phase, an Indian is ideally preparing himself for a gradual disengagement, and detachment. The death/departure is inevitable and the psychological journeys to reinvent oneself and to find new and creative ways to sublimate become essential. It is part of the mental hygiene and cultural prescription. In the west, there is no pressure to detach, relinquish and distance oneself. Existing on the margins of rat race is acceptable. For Hindus, nothing is ever outside the spirituality and that includes vanaprastha.

> *"It is the nature of desire never to be fulfilled, but he who eternally gives it up is eternally fulfilled at that very moment."*
>
> *-Tirukural 370*

Vanaprastha Contrasted with Retirement

In the Western concept of retirement, spirituality is not sought after as a focus. . The Consumption driven behavior continues as well as pursuit of finding meaning through different sort of work. Vanaprastha offers the opportunity and tools to become purpose driven, spiritually rooted, and to serve the greater cause i.e. sublimation.

Insecurity, worrying, fear, and constant pressure to keep up with daily challenges tends to be a full-time job in the Western context even after retirement. Westerners seem to always be short on time and constantly negotiating priorities and practicing multitasking. Vanaprastha allows one to feel free, live simply, and pursue detachment from it all including god, religion and materialism.

The Western context requires sense-based interaction and existence. Reality is dominated by what one sees, touches, feels, hears, tastes, thinks, or anticipates. Vanaprastha can successfully facilitate intuition-based living and meditation-based experiences. Sensory-based living tends to be reactive, up and down leaving the sympathetic nervous system exhausted. A Vanaprasthee learns to live through the parasympathetic nervous system, non-reactivity, detached action, and emotional neutrality. There is nothing to control nobody to impress and no hidden agenda nor need for an ulterior motive. One does not have to do more or try harder, but merely to allow life to happen.

Unlike the Western push to change things, improve the surrounding milieu, pursue bigger, better and more, in Vanaprastha one can choose to become free from possessions, desires, and narrow parochial loyalties. One can start preparing or living for what one always wanted to do – be free. Detachment, contentment and visualizing in the state of being in nothingness are powerful concepts to promote ultimate well-being.

If one never had a happy place, happy phase, or happy time, the Vanaprastha gives a last chance to reexamine it all and start afresh. It frees one from the obligation to be needed, approved, or defined. It allows one to begin laying the groundwork for freedom i.e. to be totally out of the box.

In Vanaprastha one gets a chance to redefine the meaning, purpose, direction, priorities, self, others, and even religiosity. One is permitted to shrug off the old and resume a new identity or even relinquish all given or chosen identities. .Often it is recommended to take new name so to have no past conditioning, caste or identity.

Vanaprastha is synonymous with making a difference internally or externally, personally or socially, resigning or restarting, and even all at once. There is no place for the status quo, stagnation, or just getting by. Vanaprastha offers the opportunity and means to rise above the mundane.

The midpoint in life does not have to be midlife crises. With some awareness and realization, it can be a peak time for sublimation. Sexuality has to be put in its proper place around this time since it offers a rather limited means to become intimate and experience joy. The desires will only lead to frustration and therefore one needs to be open to experience a higher level of maturity, not based on the senses but rather on consciousness, balance, and mindfulness.

One can afford to become the roving ambassador of service and good will by visiting various countries and attempting to make the world a better place than when first encountered. Opportunities for creative sublimation can be boundless.

Prescriptions and Proscriptions in Vanaprastha

- The rat race of Grahastha ashram where all the economic, social, and emotional drama takes place is not conducive to Vanaprastha. Grahastha ashram is nothing but a sympathetic nervous system roller coaster which is tied to negative feelings and stress. This period lasts about 25 years and that should be enough to make one tired. Distance from the familiar and routine places such as family, work, business and socialization is required. Interacting in the society in which one lived his or her earlier phases must be curtailed significantly. If one desires less or, even better, nothing, the potential for contentment increases multi-fold. Desire is the single most threatening element as it triggers the entire somato-psycho-socio-spiritual crisis (vicious cycle of like-dislike, clinging-aversion, pleasure-pain, etc.). As long as one pursues people, things, objects, and stimuli and experiences attachment, one is doomed to suffer from the endless chain of insecurity, depression, and vulnerability, anxiety, worrying, and obsessing.
- If necessary, one can return to the household one left behind from time-to-time. One can even relinquish Vanaprastha and return to one's place in the family, work, and society.
- The wife may accompany the husband in Vanaprastha and with him follow the same routine. The sexual dimension of the relationship must be moderated but not given up as in the final phase, Sanyasa.
- Fancy clothes, costly fabric, and customized tailoring must be avoided. Clothes should be made of vegetable fibers, honoring simplicity and autonomy. Nature was our original home and now we get another chance to return to it.
- Food should be vegetarian, simple, mostly consisting of plants, fruits and vegetables. One should consume one meal a day, never completely filling the stomach. One must make sure, before eating, that no one in sight is hungry. It is one's duty to invite a hungry person, whether friend or foe. Alcohol and drugs are an absolute taboo in Vanaprastha.
- Meditation, contemplation, good reading, and yoga should occupy all available leisure time. However, gardening is not prohibited.

- Adequate time should be spent teaching, helping, supporting, and nurturing others in hospitals, schools, orphanages, and other appropriate social service settings. Attaching to a temple to offer specialized services is also recommended.
- Serving society is the most important mission along with meditation, contemplation, silence, and acquiring knowledge. Ritual participation is deemphasized.
- Possessiveness for land, gold and the opposite sex has to be avoided. Ambition, desire, honors, wealth, and luxury must be curtailed. All nonessential money matters must be restricted.
- Frugality, simplicity, and contentment are essential traits to be practiced.
- Restraining anger, relinquishing pride and subordinating all negative feelings are essential in the Vanaprastha life. Buddha viewed anger as one of the three poisons along with greed and delusion. Non-reactivity is the ultimate strength of a model Vanaprasthee. Detaching from anger holds the key. Emotions of compassion and equanimity are cultivated.

Strategies for Greater Success

Especially in the complexity of the 21st century, parenting is challenging – regardless of background, ethnicity, religion, or socioeconomic status. Traditional parenting was learned and practiced as a cultural and religious role modeling. The "trial and error" approach was not very acceptable to Indians. However, with the popularity of modern psychology, worldwide exposure via media, and easy international traveling or living in foreign cultures, a great deal of confusion has prevailed. The pressure on parents to integrate psychologists' recommendations as well as some of the values and norms of traditional and modern perspectives has exacerbated the situation. As children's expectations have changed, they show clear awareness of cross-cultural and cross-religious differences. What follows is a mix of my own observations and opinions I've expressed to parents:

- Children do well when they are living in an environment with certainty, predictability, and continuity. Honesty in sharing of feelings and behavioral transparency can go a long way.
- Children have feelings which need to be listened to, acknowledged and encouraged to share and express. One should not wait for a crisis, acting out, or legal entanglements to realize the power of

feelings. They should be respected rather than judged or discouraged.

- Children may be lowest in the hierarchy, but their needs for privacy, personal space, personal preferences, likes, and dislikes are important and they should be allowed experimentation within certain boundaries.
- Relatives and religion should not be imposed on children. Their interest and involvement should be facilitated gently, gradually and with a lot of patience. They may rebel during adolescence but by their thirties they almost always return to their roots. Having patience is the best way to cope.
- Regardless of the strengths of the Indian culture, one should not think that it is the perfect culture. Children should be raised with an appreciation of the "best of both worlds."
- There is nothing wrong in having clear moral /social standards and expectations. For example it is perfectly OK to convey to children that engaging in alcohol, drug use, irresponsible sex, and making children without ensuring proper and durable parenting is not a grey area open for experimentation or compromise.
- Do not worry if your children are not your clones or if they confront you with your own inconsistencies and hypocrisies. Unlike in India, parenting involves two-way street of sharing. Let your children help you grow.
- Do not obsess with children. Stop micromanaging and living for them. Be a husband or wife, be socially active, have hobbies and a life apart from them. Help them manage their own stress rather than feeling like you have to manage it for them.
- Promote a psychological sense of separation, individuation and autonomy in your children. It will make them resilient and better able to face adversity. Your second role as they transition from childhood to adulthood is to "prepare them for the jungle" and become their teacher. This means helping them to be powerful, efficient adults and decision makers. Their eventual autonomy does not mean disloyalty or disrespect for you.
- Leave them alone in their room or personal space; let them decorate it the way they want. Do not go in the room unless it's a health hazard, filthy beyond belief or some crime is being committed. I tell parents to think that their children's rooms are like foreign countries: you can't go there unless you have a visa. It may seem too simple, but your children will respect you if you let them be free to be in their own space.

- Do not dictate their ultimate choice of profession based on your own insecurities or need for status. Chances are they will follow you anyway and, at worst, find their own way.
- Remember the only crises in life are death, disaster, fire, or cancer. The rest of the problems are just mere passing events. Promoting children's excellence is admirable, but not at the cost of their happiness, mental well-being, and health. Nothing is worth having a psychotic breakdown or coming suicide. Then you will really have a crisis.
- Imitating western parenting values is not a solution. At the same time, it's neither feasible nor worth trying to recreate the India of your childhood. Do not feel guilty: the U.S. model is not perfect. Be free to consciously design your own composite culture synthesizing the best of the east and west. But make sure it allows individuality in choices involving music, food, sports, etc. Television, video games, texting, and use of a phone should be balanced and limits set to allow other priorities to take place such as chores, helping parents or siblings, homework, exercising/yoga, learning and hobbies.
- Boredom is a common and pervasive complaint of youth. Do not feel that you have to go out of your way to provide your child sensory stimulation or allow prolonged TV or video games. First accept that boredom can be attention deficit disorder, depression, loneliness, or addiction. It is the child's responsibility to accept it, tolerate it, convey his or her needs, and finally find acceptable alternatives to address it. The strength of Indian culture is introspection, sublimation, and having an inner sanctuary. Nowhere is it said that all the five senses have to be in perpetual stimulation 24/7.

Alcoholism and Other Addictions

Yes, Indians Have Alcohol and Addiction Problems.

Pramod Patel was a 34-year-old married, Gujarat born, college-educated, father of two children, who came to the USA in 1995. He had a significant head trauma caused by an auto accident, and had been hospitalized for duodenal ulcers. He came for counseling because he had lost his job due to drinking. When I saw him, he was undergoing alcohol withdrawal. He had a total of three Driving While under the Influence (DUI/DWI) charges. In spite of legal requirements, he had never followed up in treatment, and he was in denial.

Diagnostically he suffered from alcohol dependence (alcoholism) and alcohol-related disorders. Since he was still in denial, no treatment was possible. His family was also not available to participate in treatment, which is a necessity. When someone has a problem with addiction it is not uncommon that family member or significant others tend to be enablers.

It is not only the Indian community in the United States that is experiencing the growth of alcoholism. Addictions of all sorts have become pervasive throughout the world. The addiction epidemic has crossed caste, ethnic, socio-economic, and cultural barriers. Even where the use of alcohol used to be taboo, such as in Pakistan and among the upper castes of India, alcoholism has become pervasive and even accepted.

Usually thought of as a teetotaler country, India has seen a rise in alcoholism. According to the Indian Alcohol Policy Alliance, per capita consumption of alcohol increased by 106.7% over the 15-year period from 1970 to 1996. Although alcohol use is low by world standards, 80% of alcohol consumption is in the form of hard liquor. According to the January 2009 issue of *the Lancet*, the pattern of alcohol consumption in India is frequent and heavy drinking.

A growing trend in India is to view alcohol as a symbol of being modern and a requirement for "having a good time." Drinking and driving is "macho," and any suggestion that this is a dangerous behavior is laughed at. Drinking alcohol is rationalized as being "forward" or "modern," a sign of separating oneself from the "common" or "traditional" masses, who are viewed as unsophisticated.

Indians abroad tend to be more vulnerable due to their not having developed social networks, healthy routines, and recreational options. The new waves of single Indian immigrants are from villages, barely educated and working long hours for less than minimum wages. They may live in a small group that after work cooks and shares an Indian meal and enjoys it with whiskey. They may have grown up fantasizing about the day they'd have free access to alcohol, could afford it, and could obtain it easily. They have not learned the dangers of daily drinking and have no concept of addiction. They have no awareness that there is a bigger world out here and that they have many options for socializing. They feel safe in their little space with their compatriots and live for saving some money, returning home, or eventually buying their own business.

The newcomers lack the necessary social skills for joining the mainstream. The Indian community in their adopted land offers no orientation on how to adjust in the larger community or how to be a responsible alcohol user. They never get to deal with emotional-cultural baggage they may have brought from home and unconsciously take refuge in long, hard evening drinking.

The degree to which Indians accept the use of alcohol seems to correlate with socio-economic class structure, caste order, exposure to Westernized educational institutions, and the type of family from which one comes.

Contributing factors include:

- Economic prosperity.
- Western influence via movies and the entertainment culture, and relaxed attitudes about alcohol use in general.
- Reduced influence of the extended family and accountability to the community.
- A switch in emphasis on learning from role models to the Western style of learning by trial and error, i.e., early autonomy and generational separations.
- Consumption orientation, i.e., instant gratification.
- Loss of culture-specific uniqueness through globalization of information and values, which includes intensified Proselytization of indigenous people by non-indigenous Christian missionaries who confuse culture and nationality with spirituality.

Since addictions impact health, family, work productivity, law violations, and public safety, the direct and indirect costs of addiction are beyond calculation. The fascination with alcohol and its ever increasing consumption continue in both developed and developing societies despite efforts to educate the public, modify laws, and curb marketing.

Although road fatalities and other alcohol-related impairments are increasing to the point of becoming a national epidemic, India and other developing nations have no systematic diagnostic and treatment programs for alcoholics and lack laws to handle the consequent behavior of problem drinking.

In developed countries, the severity of the problem of alcoholism and other diseases of addiction and their destructive nature has been recognized. These societies are trying to find effective ways to control and treat these diseases and contain the destruction caused by them. In the United States, voluntary organizations such as Alcoholics Anonymous (AA), Narcotics Anonymous (NA), Al-Anon (families and friends of alcoholics), Mothers Against Drunk Driving (MADD), and Students Against Drunk Driving (SADD) are multiplying to support the recovery of those who are ready to overcome their addictions. Medical and mental health professionals have accepted the challenge and are working hard to offer prevention, diagnosis, and treatment.

The Oldest Tranquilizer

Gyan was 60, had an 11th grade education, was married, and had three adult sons. His middle son suffered from Attention Deficit Hyperactivity Disorder.

Gyan originally came from an extremely deprived background and immigrated to the U.S. in 1975 with the help of a Christian missionary. His wife's family also traveled from India to live with him. Gyan worked hard, and did quite well financially; eventually he retired with good health and pension benefits.

However, he suffered from severe diabetes, high cholesterol, insomnia, and was blind in one eye. He had been an alcoholic for over 30 years. He was under the care of a psychiatrist and other specialists, and was taking a variety of medications for his health complications.

He preferred drinking rum, usually four shots a day alone at home. He obsessively complained that his wife sided with her mother and her brother. This made him very angry as he felt abandoned. He had chronic marital problems, and his wife eventually gave up on him. He came to seek help only because his wife threatened to put him in jail, and he felt scared. His wife wanted to separate from him, but he didn't want to. His life revolved around his wife, children, home, and money making, and he had no other life and was ill prepared for changes in his life.

Diagnostically, he suffered from alcohol dependence (alcoholism), marital problems, and parent-child problems. Psycho-dynamically, in spite of his denials, rationalizations, and pattern of blaming others, his problems revolved around alcoholism. He grew up as an orphan and seemed destined to end up as an orphan, all alone. His wife and children lost all respect for him. The harder he tried to cling to the family, the more alienated he felt. He was really not open to psychological or alcohol treatment and thus kept relapsing. The last I heard, his depression had worsened, he had become blind totally and was divorced.

A Hindu View of Addictions

Indians do not view addiction as a disease but as a habituated desire. This desire is viewed as the core of all pathology. Giving in to desire and acting on desire "fuel the fire." Desire is the core of all human suffering, operating through human senses. Most of the early psychologists have affirmed the role of senses in pathology; however, the concept of desire is originally Hindu. Western psychology only now is recognizing the role of desire in human pathology and suffering.

Addictions come as a cluster or a syndrome and never alone. This is due to the fact that desire inevitably needs and uses the five senses, and, notably, all the orifices of the body. Following the Western model, it is no longer enough to simply and separately enjoy the pleasures of eating, drinking, entertainment, and sexual relations. The psycho-dynamics of alcoholism, drug and food addictions, object and attachment obsessions, and sexually deviant behaviors, can be explained effectively in the desire model of emotional drive.

Society can hold on to the ideals of male-female virginity. However, the desires and in particular sexual urges often drive human behavior. Mere religion, moral ideals, or even sublimation cannot prevent sexual acting out, desires, or preoccupation. Denials or evasiveness only further complicate the relationships between genders. The best options are to own human sexuality as a powerful reality, promote sublimation, provide education and skills to meet sexual needs appropriately, and yet hold on to the social ideals as they work like a prophylactic and promote exceptional growth. Deviancy, psychopathy, perversions, sexual violence like rape should be treated like any other crime.

Happiness is a state of mind in which one is content and free from the perpetual pull of the senses and the push of desire. In the traditional Hindu view, the goal of life is not to pursue pleasure (serving the senses), but to become totally free from the bondage of pleasure and the pain. For consumption-oriented, free-market Western economics to survive, addictions are essential. The individual response to this materialistic imperative is depression, withdrawal, and aggression, acting out, phobias, perversions, panic attacks, obsessive-compulsive disorder, and character disorders. Pleasure and pain are tied together in addiction: pleasure leads to addiction, and that leads to pain.

Treatment Options for Non-Western Alcoholics

Currently, the most effective approach to the treatment of alcoholism is found in the wisdom of Alcoholics Anonymous (AA), a program based on action and spiritually. If the techniques of Hindu psychology are added to the principles of AA, the combined approach not only would treat addictions successfully, it could be used to create happiness and even Nirvana.

Although Alcoholics Anonymous offers the best hope for the treatment and rehabilitation of alcoholics, its success rate ranges between 30 and 40 percent. Western psychology and medicine have proven to be of little value in the rehabilitation of alcoholics, leaving 60 to 70 percent of alcoholics without any hope. Non-Western and many Western addicts resist AA. They and their families suffer in utter helplessness. With the majority of active alcoholics not being treated effectively, exploring and applying other approaches and cross-cultural methods are of critical importance.

Therapy should focus on the following:

- Helping the patient become more sensitive and aware of objective reality, confronting him with facts, statistics, and second opinions.
- Strengthening the patient's capacity to confront his weaknesses and deficiencies.
- Helping the patient identify and productively use his or her gifts and strengths.
- Helping the patient develop less pretentious and illusory attitudes and behaviors.
- Helping the patient develop realistic and spiritually-based insights and behaviors.
- Treating the co-morbid pathology of addiction. For example, depression in many cases is the co-morbid condition behind the addiction. For Indians, it may be difficult to perceive depression as many do not allow themselves to "feel feelings." In this case, alcohol use masks the underlying depression.

Therapeutic methods that can be employed include:

- Letter-writing. Talking does not happen easily. Moreover some people are not that creative. I think it is much more effective if the significant others were to write letters to the addict. Letters should be honest, thoughtful, and direct and can be even confrontational.

It gives everybody room to save face, convey their exact feelings and concerns, and above all, give time to process.

- Environmental management. Change the association of "people, places, and things" to environments where alcohol or drug consumption is absent.
- Psychopharmacological intervention. Medications such as Antabuse, Dolophin, Revex, Narcan, and Buprenex can help manage the condition.
- Behavior modification. There are a number of techniques aimed at teaching the patient to transform self-destructive behaviors into productive, health-generating ones.
- Cognitive reorientation and introspection. The goal is to help patients recognize, interrupt, and redirect their addiction compulsions.
- Family therapy. To promote a realistic view of self and learning interpersonal skills of frankness and assertiveness without fearing disapproval and shame.
- Identifying passive-aggressive or dependent personality disorders. These require longer-term treatment.
- Offering orientation courses. These can be offered to Diaspora newcomers in Hindu temples (Mandirs). The orientation's goal should be to promote healthy acculturation and address socialization skills.
- Re-create healthy homeland imitations (Little Indias). Immigrants are likely to do this in some form, but can be encouraged to strengthen these inward havens as a means of sustaining their Indian identity without the risk of alcoholism, drug dependence, or acting out. They can re-create their homelands through simple practices such as speaking their language, listening to familiar music, and cooking native meals.

Twelve-Step Alternative

Without a doubt, the most effective treatment method for people struggling with various forms of addiction is a recovery group that employs a Twelve-Step Program.

The major concern that I have with these programs is that, contrary to their assertion, they constitute a religious-like system. AA and recovery movements are false religions with false religious systems, attempting to lead mankind to a better and happier life. During my clinical practice for the past 40 years, I have had many individuals who were unable to relate or participate in this model.

There is a profound difference between spirituality and religion. Thus, I propose the following application of the Twelve-Step Program incorporating Sankhya-Yoga philosophy, which is derived from Hindu philosophy.

1. We proclaim to others and ourselves that what we perceive as "selves" is only a drop in the ocean upon which we are dependent and with which we are integrated. We come to realize and believe that ego (I, me, and mine) must go, be stripped, and melted.

2. This ocean is the body and spirit of the Supreme Being, the Creator. To deny this or not recognize it as such places us in a state of disengagement with our Source of life and wisdom. We must realize that all desires must be surrendered to and governed by spirituality.

3. We desire to spiritually and physically acknowledge and worship the Supreme Being and defer arrogance of personally acquired "wisdom" to him and his prophets, luminaries, and writers, which we will study. We know the best place to begin such study is with the best and direct sources of our spiritual heritage, beginning at their origin. We come to realize that in order to experience the higher self and the universal spirit, we must look after others, and nurture the weak and vulnerable.

4. We will continually meditate on the status of our spiritual development and gauge it according to the enlightened teachings of our spiritual directors and spiritual heritage. We commit to take full responsibility for our karma.

5. In the devotion to the Step 4 practice, we are willing and anxious to recognize the status of our spiritual development and vow to grow through further development. We believe that we must overcome our character defects by learning, understanding, integrating, and living a Satvic life.

6. In the devotion to the Step 5 practice, we are willing and anxious to nurture our spiritual development, even if it involves devotion to studying the scriptures of our spiritual heritage and seeking guidance from spiritual directors. We will stop behaviors like excesses of eating, sleeping, working, socializing, talking and, even thinking, partaking of them only what's needed to sustain health and life.

7. We will use our abilities in reading, listening, writing (journaling), and self-expression through art, music, and dialog with others. We will engage in daily discipline, detoxification of our bodies (yama),

training our minds (niyama), and seek company of persons grounded in spirituality (satvik).

8. We will make amends to those we have harmed or harbor negative feelings towards, so long as this is not aimed primarily toward making us feel better or self-righteous. We will practice sankhya-yoga, acquire wisdom, and improve personal integration via actions and service without ulterior motives (nishkam seva).

9. We will continue to live in a manner that does not cause injury to others and ourselves in thoughts, feelings, and actions. We will see oneness in all and so work to nurture it all.

10. We will continue to regularly reflect upon progress in the practice of the previous steps. We will seek an experienced, spiritually sophisticated mentor for guidance.

11. We now submit ourselves to the Highest Power in pursuit of our spirituality. We will continue to practice humility so as to become free from arrogance and ignorance that would interfere with our personal growth and our preparation to serve others.

12. We will not impose on others, remembering the dredges from which we came and the importance of continual practice of humility. Having realized the value of spirituality, we will devote our lives and energy to it by serving others.

The Indian Psychopath

The Diagnostic and Statistical Manual of Mental Disorders IV (DSM) in essence describes psychopaths, sociopaths, and those with antisocial personalities as people who lack all empathy with others. They do not abide by the social, religious, or legal norms, and are utterly self-centered. These individuals may use people, lie, have a choppy job history, have a criminal record, and can inflict violence on others. Promiscuity and drug/alcohol abuse is also not uncommon.

However, due to cultural variables, Indian psychopaths do not always have criminal records, have a pattern of drug or alcohol abuse, and engage in promiscuity or practice violence. They are harder to detect because these individuals resort to using various professional or cultural disguises. They may have religious titles such as *panda* (Hindu scholar), *pujari* (Hindu priest), *maulwi* (Muslim religious scholar) or *imam* (Muslim priest). They may also hide behind professional roles and layers of bureaucracy and be clerks, police, government employees, politicians, physicians, and jurists. Psychopathy comes to play in relationships, friendships, or when one encounters individuals during transitions, such as traveling, on pilgrimages, etc. A typical transaction will start with the psychopath asking a small favor but then escalating the request into a full-fledged one, such as borrowing a large sum of money or expecting to be sponsored to come abroad. Sometimes, the initial contact will be a plea for help with needing money for school, college, or to pay off a loan. But then the game will exacerbate, and the request will be repeated again and again. The irony is that it all takes place without any shame, gratitude, or consideration for the helper's feelings or limitations. If the helper acquiesces, it will usually end with the helper losing money, relationships, and all further contact.

Non-resident Indians are most vulnerable for being used and exploited by psychopaths when they come as guests, relatives, or as co-workers or business partners. An Indian friend once had invited his former professor from India to stay with him in Pennsylvania. He gave him his own bedroom to sleep in. After his departure, the friend received a very high phone bill because the professor was making all his international calls throughout the entire night of his stay. Another friend experienced a different version when his former professor made the NRI host pay for all his shopping including the caviar that he was taking to India. Other reported experiences include items being stolen, money being borrowed, and getting drunk on the host's liquor.

The following describes the characteristics of the Indian psychopath:

- Charming, overly polite, down to earth, exaggerated modesty in outward behavior.
- Language is carefully chosen to come across as honest, trustworthy, simple, and without any agendas or ulterior motives.
- The tone and quality of voice is the master clue. Psychopaths will ensure that their voice is tender, soft, gentle, polite, non-assertive, and almost boyish and feminine during communication. This tone is used to prepare the ground for a follow up surprise or demand for a favor. It's a remarkable tool utilized most efficiently to disarm you so that you cannot dare say no.
- Physical appearance is highly conventional, religious or prim-and-proper, and calculated to create an image of being authentic, genuine, and reassuring.
- Underneath this facade, the Indian psychopath is highly calculating, utterly selfish, and constantly maneuvering. The Indian word for maneuvering is *jugad*. The interesting aspect is that jugad

and hustling, manipulating, and testing others never stops. Your space is constantly invaded and any and all contact proves injurious to the weak.

- He never honors commitments, contracts, or agreed-upon terms and conditions.
- She privately engages in hedonistic pleasures such as drinking or gluttonous eating.
- He exhibits lack of empathy and is driven by the promise of material gain. Lying, cheating, and bribes may be a means to an end.
- She goes out of the way to appear accommodating, but underneath schemes to steal, take advantage, or set the victim up in some complex triangle to gain benefit.
- He may engage in very controlled and highly sneaky sexual exploits, while claiming to be pious, pure, or religious.
- Indian ethnic newspapers are replete with news of Indian's psychopathic behavior, ranging from committing identity fraud to hiring contract killers. India Abroad reported on September 5, 2014 that a self-proclaimed Guru, Annamalai, was convicted on 34 felony counts. On August 1, 2014 an Indian-American CEO was convicted of paying kick-backs. Indian psychopaths commit varieties of criminal behavior ranging from duping and trafficking Indian women, attempting murder, immigration scam, slavery, falsifying identity, kidnapping, and more.

It's Not Me, Everyone Else is Crazy

Gayatri was a 45-year-old, Chennai-born Hindu female. She had an adolescent son and a daughter, and her husband was a computer professional. She had two masters' degrees and was employed until the birth of her son. She had been married, arranged-style, for 20 years. Her daughter was doing well in college while the son was living home and showed severe dysfunction in terms of being immature, angry, and underperforming in school.

Gayatri preferred to see me alone. During the session she presented herself as "all together," in control of her life and put the blame on her daughter and husband. She was worried about her son while she described her daughter as being a slut and alcoholic. However, probing through other sources revealed that she has been irrational, paranoid, psychotic, and for long time, impossible in her mother and wife roles. She had many consultations but was always noncompliant, both with following up as well as taking medications. She'd often impulsively leave her family and go to India for prolonged periods. She acted violently towards her husband and the police become involved. The court restricted her involvement with the children.

She was suffering from schizophrenia, paranoid-type, with brief psychotic episodes, marital problems, and parent-child relational problems.

Right after the initial session, she went to India for an indefinite period. Occasionally, she sent me emails worrying about her son, and whether he kept his appointments. However, her husband had an excuse that the son did not want to come for counseling.

Delusional Disorder

DSM-IV defines delusional disorder as non-psychotic, somewhat reality based misconception-of-self behavior that is without any significant impairment of functioning. This behavior may be accompanied with tactile or olfactory hallucinations. Types of delusional disorder are based on themes. These include the following types: erotomanic, grandiose, jealous, persecutory, somatic, mixed type, or unspecified.

Anecdotally speaking, the grandiose type is the most prominent among Indians. It manifests in social situations and is accompanied by the overwhelming need to impress others. Typically, Indians' statements pertain to the following themes:

- Indian medicine (Ayurveda) system is perfect and better than all other systems of medicine.
- India is the best country in the whole world. Its people are superior and are the most modest, simple, loving, and kind. This belief is rooted in the need to prove that Western/European cultures are not as good, kind, sincere, and honest as Indian culture.
- Indian civilization is the oldest and is the most evolved.

The Thousand Faces of Fear

Abdul was a 33-year-old single, U.S. raised Muslim who lived with his parents and younger brother. His sister was married and lived on her own. His mother was a housewife, and his father a physician. When Abdul was attending medical school he had his own apartment.

He had consulted a few psychiatrists, but had not responded well to medications. He came to see me sporadically and was able to trust and comply. He was suffering a great deal but had avoided psychological counseling. His symptoms included severe impairment as to attention, concentration, focusing, obsessive compulsivity, phobias, fears, social anxiety, bouts of extreme rage, irrational acting behavior, putting himself and the family in danger, having unreasonable grandiose demands from his father, and catastrophizing and anticipating doom and gloom. He stalked his girlfriend and felt could not survive without clinging to her.

He was suffering from Bipolar Disorder II, mixed, rapid cycling, obsessive compulsive disorder, and parent-child conflict. His delusional disorder was the erotomanic type.

Psycho-dynamically his fear of separation, independent living, and entrance to an adult role evoked a pervasive sense of helplessness and an anticipation of failure. His demanding, clinging, aggressive behavior towards his father was actually a cover-up for his intense fear and lack of self-confidence. He did not trust his feelings or faculties, with regard to seeing, hearing, interacting, judgment, and decision making.

He responded well to individual and family psychotherapy and acquired skills for identifying, tolerating, and verbalizing his feelings (happiness, sadness, anger, fear, anxiety, and jealousy). In spite of being Muslim, his family respected his interest in yoga, occasional alcohol use, and having Hindu friends. Eventually he married, and transitioned into a remarkable adulthood.

Indians as Mental Health Consumers

"The sorrow which has no vent in tears may take other organs weep." - Henry Maudsley

As a consumer, the Indian patient is minimally aware, totally uninvolved, and rarely reaches out. In the words of S.A., an Indian patient, "Indian people do not take mental health professionals seriously, and fear stigma and social ostracism." He felt that in most Indian families, the head of the household handles "in-house" major conflicts relating to relationships. Regardless of the source of the conflict, Indians do not trust an outsider's opinion. S.A. suggested that the Indian consumer needs to be educated on the nature of the mental health profession, the benefits of counseling, and the consequences of not seeking help.

As it inherently implies that they have failed and are weak, an Indian patient's decision to consult a mental health professional is an overwhelming experience. It also exacerbates their sense of vulnerability and loss of control. Feeling emotions and processing them is an unfamiliar concept for Indians, since they have been taught since birth to suppress, repress, or conceal them. Indians mostly *intellectualize* instead of *recognizing and owning* their feelings, whether sorrow, anger, fear, or worry. They approach life as a task and their coping mechanism is invariably robotic or mechanical.

Denial: Hindus even have a word for it called *maya*, meaning all of creation is nothing but an illusion due to its perpetually changing nature. This is the perfect example of profound denial. Everything is transient and therefore nothing is to be taken seriously but merely observed dispassionately. This mindset is not limited to spirituality, but goes into dealing with suffering, emotional or otherwise. Besides lacking information about the utility of mental health services, denial is a major factor that prevents Indians from seeking help.

This denial mechanism is rather complex, as it makes Indians not see the problem, imagining it will automatically disappear. Denial involves engaging in elaborate rationalizations, simplifications, oversimplifications, or inappropriate remedial measures. Indians invented cognitive-behavioral therapy without ever calling it so. They define desire as the cause of all suffering and therefore confront themselves to annihilate it by seeing all objective reality as maya, or choosing detachment.

Take the case of Vineet (who had a 10-year-old daughter from a previous marriage) and a second wife who felt abandoned, depressed, agitated and withdrawn. They came to get help because the school noticed that the daughter was having bruises and was suffering from malnourishment. When they came to see me, they had already decided to ship the girl to a boarding school in India. The father and the grandfather's logic was that she would get a good spiritual education in the Indian cultural context. It took only a few sessions to identify that the step-mother was redirecting her own desperation to the daughter to get back at the husband, since she was trapped in caring for her own infant and step-daughter, while not receiving any adult attention. Only after a few sessions the entire family developed a very open communication and the entire crisis ended. Follow-up marriage therapy sessions continued since the husband lacked the skill to empathize with his wife and address her emotional needs.

Shipping the children to live with grandparents or family members in India and schooling there is a common practice among Gujarati immigrants. It does not take into consideration the child's feelings, emotional needs and attachments with parents and peers.

Social Situations: Indians have serious difficulty in curtailing and altering their private behavior while in social situations. They see the social aspect as an extension of the personal space and private world, which causes them to pay a heavy price.

Cultural crossfire: Indians in India do not face the same confusion, self-doubts, or obsess with the issue of "Who am I?" These issues become very prominent and emotionally draining for Indians who are living abroad and have to interact with other cultures, values, or expectations. I recall in a social gathering an Indian aptly jokingly saying, "My wallet is here, but my heart is in India."

Let's take the case of the young Indian man who was arrested by the police for walking nude on the median of the Garden State Parkway in New Jersey. When he was brought to the hospital where I worked, he stated that he was "walking the middle of the road," meaning acting out his ambivalence, confusions, and conflicts about being an Indian and having to live in America, and not being able to emotionally reconcile the two.

Even though Indian Diaspora population has rapidly increased and almost all major cities have "Little Indias", and Indian communities have become concentrated, Indians continue to feel split between India and their host countries, and between Eastern and Western values. The result sometimes manifests as emotional distress and disorders such as engaging in crimes, being ticketed for DUI, or acting out at work.

Self-insulation: Indians have a difficult time accepting feelings of vulnerability, not being in control, being exposed, or being the center of attention. They insulate themselves to buffer from feelings of inadequacy or incompetence. The cover-up can involve resorting to alcohol, an obsession with money, excessive religiosity, or more complex masking, such as intellectual pursuits, professional preoccupations, and grandiosity. It is not uncommon for Indians who self-insulate to glorify India at the expense of the countries in which they live.

Externalizers: The opposite of self-insulators are the externalizers who have difficulty dealing with their feelings, coping with alienation, and being in unfamiliar situations. Such persons may engage in social drinking, visit gentleman's clubs, and might even show up on the NBC show "To Catch a Predator."

Over Protectiveness: By and large Indian parents find it very difficult to tolerate their children or adolescents' separation and autonomy. They use education as a tool to exercise control to protect their children from exposure to risky behavior. Although this has its usefulness, it also adds to children's stress and hinders them finding balance between their home culture and the outside world.

Indian parents show extreme fear of their children dating or exploring their sexuality. The parents of a fifth grader brought him to see me because of poor academic performance. When I evaluated him, it became very clear that he was suffering from a learning disability and also had ADHD. Following the feedback, the parents became non-compliant to treatment. I later learned that they had "solved" the problem by relocating to a different school district.

Masking the symptoms: Indians have difficulty dealing with mental disorders such as depression and alcoholism due to their sense of failure and of being weak. They tend to be extremely self-critical but also naive as to the nature of the disease and the value of professional help. They also deal with their internal conflicts by avoiding any association or affiliation with their religion, community, and country. Their aversion tends to be highly exaggerated and extreme and may manifest by their choosing to Americanize or Christianize their names, and by disowning anything Indian.

Obsessive compulsivity: Although Alcoholics Anonymous invented the approach of "Keeping It Simple, Stupid," Indians have perfected it by limiting their focus to being driven towards professional perfection and business entrepreneurship, earning and hoarding money. This is a kind of obsessive-compulsive disorder that is an Indian trademark.

Even after getting married, Indians tend to obsessively cling to parents and siblings who might be thousands of miles away, as shown by daily or weekly long-distance calls, sending money to them regularly and failing to entertain their spouses. At the same time, they might micromanage their spouses and children with the aim of protecting them from any unforeseen, unimaginable crisis.

External locus of control: On one hand, Indians like to be in control to avoid feeling vulnerable. But on the other hand, they relinquish their sense of control by handing it over to others. Indians' need for approval, validation, acknowledgement, testimonials, and compliments by others is an ever-present phenomenon. It is not good enough for Indians to be proud of their Vedas, Indian medicine, vegetarianism or an Indian female being an astronaut, unless and until Westerners, or the English media acknowledge it. The Indian sense of power being externally located creates a paradoxically opposite stereotype of being seen as meek, weak, complacent, insecure, and people pleasing.

The following letter by a 39-year-old female psychotherapy patient conveys the essence of therapeutic journey.

My Dear Greesh,

Trying to write my feelings in a letter is like packing the ocean into a water bottle. I could not be more grateful to the universe for allowing my path to cross yours. As a therapist, you were the solid ground that kept me standing when my entire world crumbled around me. Before I started my therapy I thought I was a smart cookie who had figured out the world and its intricacies. I came begrudgingly for the first few months. I kept coming back as a challenge - to prove you wrong. You challenged as no one else had before in your kind, wise, and gentle manner. I found myself relearning the world and its workings from you. You have taught me to value myself when I thought I had no value. You have shared light on every corner of my life and helped me put it in perspective. You started as a challenge and I have become now my own therapist and healer. You will always be one and only Guru.

December 16, 2014

Modern Mental Health Solutions

Western psychology has a very short history of roughly 100 years. Its origin can be traced to Germany specifically and Europe generally, and is basically reflective of the Caucasian, European mindset, personality, and interpersonal relationship patterns. By implication, it is limited and incongruent to the personal and interpersonal dynamics of individuals from other continents, cultural contexts, religions, and societies. India's culture in particular is a great example of this incongruence and incompatibility.

As it developed in the West, psychology was a by-product of the two world wars. In other words, it has its origin in crisis, violence (aggression), distrust, the struggle to stay alive, preventing alienation, and sustaining individual identity. Obviously, two world wars created significant disruption of the family and in social, economic, and even religious aspects of the society. Western psychology evolved to meet these challenges not only by developing sophisticated concepts such as identity, individuality, separation, and individuation but also by providing clinical procedures to address neurosis, psychosis, acting out, depression, panic disorder, and phobias. Although it has made great achievements, Western psychology has limitations that to a great extent stem from its early founders attempt to establish it as a rigorously scientific field, akin to biology and physics.

Among these limitations:

- *Reductionism* or dissecting the human experience into separate parts, such as Id, Ego, Superego, Child, Adult, and Parent. Treating a human as the sum of its disparate parts is not adequate to describe the totality of the human essence.
- *An overemphasis on defense mechanisms.* These are often crudely viewed as the only mechanisms that sustain the human mind. But it is a mistake to view defense mechanisms as the sole and primary drivers of human experience. Hindu culture presents an alternative approach that emphasises disengagement, detachment, and relinquishing control.
- *The cult of the individual.* The individual is given the central role and thus his/her and I/Me/Mine become the primary frame of reference. This leads to "You and I," "Yours and Mine," and "I am for me and I need to make sure I am in control, so you don't come to grab what is mine." The implication is that I have to be alert, vigilant, powerful, assertive, protective and defensive, i.e., to exist

in a survival mode. By contrast, the Hindu approach takes the survival mode for granted and is more preoccupied with rising above the mundane and the ordinary.

- *Defining reality as something concrete.* Reality in the West is defined as something very concrete and to be taken with the utmost seriousness. An alternate approach is to define this reality as illusory, transitory, perpetually reshaping, and therefore not worthy of attachment or seriousness.

- *An overemphasis on autonomy.* The Western goal in life is to master the environment, ensure physical survival, and develop personal competence to meet individual needs. Western values are autonomy, personal space, and processing reality via the senses. Easterners in general are more collective-oriented and value the needs of the extended family over those of the individual.

- *The primacy of feelings.* To the Western mind, feelings are the primary means to experience the self, the other, the external world, and everything else. The Eastern mind sees feelings as the ultimate barriers to becoming truly objective, neutral, and free from it all.

- *Action/*Reaction. The Western mind deals with stimulation by responding to it and perfecting a strategy to balance it. An alternate approach is to practice non-reaction, and thus avoid the formation of habits that stem from reactions to stimuli. We all know that modern day psychologists make their living by helping people deal with their bad habits. Capitalism needs people to have habits so that they will remain consumers. Keeping consumers in perpetual crisis of needing more keeps the economy going. Every product becomes tied to ego, self-esteem, neediness, and "success."

Opposites of Western & Eastern Orientation

Western psychologists who treat patients from the East need to keep in mind differences between their own perspective and that of their patients.

Western	Eastern
Fight or flight	Non-reactivity
Processing of hearing, seeing, tasting and smelling	Turning off the senses
Stimuli dependence	Emotional equanimity
Arousal/sensory basis	Letting it pass
Externally driven/dependent	Silent/inward focus
Emphasis on talking	Fasting from speaking
Need to be logical	Experiencing the experience
Perfection of defense mechanisms	Stripping oneself of all defenses

Goal directed	Living in the moment
Happiness in sensory gratification	Contentment, equilibrium
Movement/action, decision	Quiet passivity, reflection
Focused on being productive and accomplished	Focused on just being
Emphasis on materialism	Detachment from possessions
Stress is a prerequisite to being alive	Stress is pathological
Problem solving by decision-making	Problem solving by quieting the mind
Reality defined by senses and logic	The only reality is there is no reality
Mind is the seat of control	Mind is a servant of the senses
Control is essential	Control is a burden/irrelevant
Desiring and satisfying	Giving in to desires begins pathology
Emotions are important	Emotions are a good tool but ultimately a burden
Personal responsibility	Collective responsibility
Individual needs are most important	Individual needs are subordinate to family and significant others
Identity is a result of trial and error	Identity evolves by role modeling and passing through critical phases
Emphasis on nuclear family	Extended family dictates
Logic and rationality are emphasized	Intuition and instinct are nurtured
Emotions are to be dealt with pragmatically	Emotions must be subordinated to duty
Play, leisure are important	No separation between play and work: it's all one
Time is vital and controls living	Time is viewed as circular and not to be taken seriously
Individual freedom of choice	Choice is imposed by family/community
One is responsible for making things happen	Things are destined
Guilt for personal failure	No major crisis or guilt
World is viewed as real	World is viewed as transitory and an illusion
Hypocrisy/contradictions are distressing	It's all seen as a paradox
Reality is sense-based	Sense-based "reality" is non-reality

When treating a patient with an Indian orientation, it's helpful to use concepts of a Vedic psychology, an approach that builds on the rich philosophical and psychological traditions of India, as captured in that country's indigenous texts such as The Upanishads and the philosophical schools of Vedānta, Sāṁkhya, Yoga, Nyāya, Vaiśeṣika and dissenting systems like Jainism and Buddhism.

Vedic Psychology

Vedic psychotherapy embodies the oldest known clinical procedures used to help human beings deal with their feelings as well as the dilemmas of life, death, growth, and Nirvana (liberation). While aspects of Vedic psychology have been incorporated by Western schools of psychotherapy, its essence is fundamentally different. For example, its closest Western counterparts – Rational-Emotive Therapy (RET), Cognitive Behavioral Therapy (CBT), and Behavior Modification – have a single-minded focus. In contrast, Vedic psychotherapy simultaneously addresses cognitive restructuring, habit and behavior changes, and the integration of spirituality.

There are five specific goals in the practice of Vedic psychotherapy:

1. Because most emotional problems correlate with the tamasik (impulsive, short-sighted, and self-centered) and rajasik (materialistic, and pleasure-oriented) traits of personality, a fundamental goal is to help the person to develop a satvik disposition rooted in the search for mindful living, individual-social, internal- external harmony, and the pursuit of spirituality. Spirituality is defined elsewhere.
2. The philosophy of Sankhya (described below) is introduced gradually as a means of promoting conceptual understanding, cognitive restructuring, habit cessation, and managing day-to-day life situations with a sense of equanimity.
3. Yoga techniques are taught to integrate the mind and body, the internal with the external, and the physical with the spiritual. The usual positive side effects of engaging in Sankhya Yoga include freedom from struggle, pain, and depression.
4. The concept of the four Ashrams (stages of life) is introduced as a framework for recognizing, labeling, organizing and facing life's demands, responsibilities, and priorities.
5. The psychology of desires and the dynamics of living a life consumed with attachments are explained. The necessity and the skills of sublimation are taught to turn the perpetual highs and lows, pain-pleasure, boredom-excitement, and action-reaction vicious cycles into living a life of meaning, purpose, and self-

actualization. Learning to overcome negative emotions like anxiety, worrying, fear, anger, sadness, and jealousy are addressed via value clarification, conceptual restructuring, self-confrontation, where higher purposes and spirituality are pursued. In other words, sublimation and emotional equanimity become important steps for self-help and personal transformation.

Essential Concepts of Vedic Psychotherapy

There are six essential concepts:

Sankhya-Yoga is the school of philosophical psychology founded by Maharishi Patanjali, who compiled the Yoga Sutras approximately two hundred years before the birth of Christ. Sankhya is the theory of Yoga and Yoga is the practice of Sankhya. Without the theory, practice alone is inadequate; without practice, theory is inadequate. Yoga follows the eight steps of *Yama* (regulations to control and discipline the lower instincts in human beings), *Niyama* (observances which help to develop a cultured and civilized life), Asana (yogic exercisers and postures), Pranayama (the art of regulating the breathing), Prityahara (process of negation), Dharna Dhyan (Meditation), and Samadhi (deep meditation).

Ashram. As discussed earlier, Hinduism prescribes four phases or Ashrams as a schedule of life: Brahmacharya (period of student life and learning), Grahstha (period of householder), Vanaprastha (period for giving back to society and related social welfare activities), and Sanyasa (period of renunciation).

Personality. Each individual has a unique constellation of traits. However, each personality has a preponderance of specific traits:

The *Tamasik* person is impulsive, short-sighted, and self-centered. In Western psychology, such personality is labeled antisocial and narcissistic. A person who has a Tamasik personality is a concrete person, governed by basic biological needs, indulging in eating meat and using alcohol. He is not simply a non-vegetarian but prefers the sour taste and leftover food. The Tamasik individual is impulsive, shortsighted, and self-centered.

Rajasik personality traits are preponderantly hedonistic, materialistic, and pleasure-oriented. However, the person with this personality would also be more resourceful and insightful than the Tamasik person.

The *Satvik* in essence means the procedures for mastering sympathetic nervous system from controlling the body and mind. Satvik Personality is consciously organized around becoming free from the perpetual yo-yo dance between sympathetic and parasympathetic nervous systems. Satvikta is the pursuit of spirituality, by using body-mind-self as an instrument for personal transformation. Identity for a wise person is not gender, ethnicity, religion nationality, time, place, possessions based but paradoxically it's universal only when one relinquishes the need to have an identity. The Satvik person is able to retrain his or her mind, turn it inward, and detach from the senses and yet be totally ion the moment.

Satvik traits include minimalism, surrender and acceptance, the pursuit of contentment and self-realization, and living in the moment without any anticipation or expectation. Ignorance, capriciousness, laziness, or jealousy and attachments are viewed as obstructions. Quiet is preferred over talking, fasting is preferred over feasting, and stillness is preferred over hurrying.

An individual may not completely embody all the traits of any one personality type. It is more likely that some traits may overlap with another personality type or change during the socialization process.

- Happiness. The concept of Happiness in Vedic psychology is different from pleasure, sense based stimulation or simply being aroused/stimulated. Drives and habits fueled by desires result eventually in bondage and suffering, a condition that is exactly the opposite of happiness. The prerequisites for arriving at the state of happiness are an absence of ambivalence and duality, a focus on the here and now, and freedom from expectations and anticipations. Nirvana is the ultimate happiness and it means "freedom from it all i.e. attachments, operating out of likes and dislikes, or needing to belong to any "ism or religion". Everything else is the beginning of the never ending cycle of either pleasure or pain.
- The Big Picture. Contradiction and paradoxes are accepted as being part of The Big Picture, which is perpetually evolving, unfolding, being born, and dying. Understanding this ebb and flow is emphasized over the compulsion to change situations. Accepting universal interconnectedness and oneness is emphasized over the need to isolate, separate, compete, or become attached to one's ego.
- Actions/Karma. Selfish karma, driven by ulterior motives, always leads to attachment and its negative consequences. Actions must be selfless, without attachment or anticipating or expecting anything.

The principles and practices of Vedic psychology offer an efficient, effective, and comprehensive psycho-somato-socio-spiritual approach for good mental hygiene and harmonious day-to-day living. It also provides the framework for genuine personality transformation either via total self-help or under the mentorship of a Guru. It is the same as psychotherapy; just the lingo is different, as well as some procedures.

The Vedic and Sankhya yoga approach to mental hygiene approaches the individual as a whole i.e. mind-body-environment and spirituality. It does not infinitely divide human beings into minute particles, symptoms or traits. This is a very cost effective approach and as result often the problems of addictions, negative habits and lifestyle, low self-esteem, and interpersonal conflicts become insignificant, and symptoms often disappear spontaneously. Of course, these approaches are not applicable when someone is in crisis such as intoxication, mental breakdown, episode or mania, in case of suicidal behavior.

Self-Help Solutions

For the most part, our emphasis has been on explaining the nature of emotional dysfunctions and psycho-therapeutic solutions to the mental health issues for Diaspora Indians. Help from professionals, whether psychiatrists, psychologists or social workers involves availability, access, insurance coverage or payment on your own. Often, even if one finds a qualified professional, it does not mean that – as patient – one will have the right "chemistry" of feeling connected, patiently treated or the ability to have an appointment when one feels the need for it. We'd be remiss if we did not acknowledge that formal treatment is simply not a practical option for many for a number of reasons:

- It may be beyond the financial means of all economic classes.
- Consulting a professional is seen, culturally, as a taboo by Indians.
- There is an extreme shortage of therapists even in metropolitan cities not to mention distant towns and remote villages.
- A qualified mental health professional does not mean degrees and license but equally important that they have through understanding of the patient's background, culture, religion and limitations of transport and affordability to buy medications.
- People often lack skills to verbalize their symptoms, define their crisis and command respect, empathy and consideration as they see the doctor "all powerful and up in hierarchy.
- People lack information as to their mental health treatment options.
- Doctors often prescribe medications without warning the patient as to potential side effects. Patient is expected to come again and again and pay for the appointments even for minor questions and concerns.
- Doctors usually do not allow access by phone, reply to letters, etc. leaving the patient in "dark".
- Mental health professionals and doctors in Third World countries do not display proof of their being qualified, having expertise and genuine.
- Local medical professionals often fail to be gatekeepers, either because they lack knowledge, are too lazy and insecure to refer to other specialists, or lack awareness as to where these specialists are available. There are lot of charlatans who practice medicine and therapy under different professional disguises and titles.
- Often exorbitant fees are charged without any explanation, advance notice or open discussion.

Being in the role of a mental health consumer, one needs to understand that professionals are not above accountability, transparency or responsibility to be ethical. They offer a service similar to any other professional like a carpenter, electrician, teacher or a government bureaucrat, and are paid for it. Patents and doctors are equal partners in the process of diagnosing, treating and properly discharging the patient. It's the doctor's moral obligation to suggest to the patients how to help themselves, what the most cost effective options are, and what other specialists need to be approached. Without such a team approach which should include, spouse, parents, children and family, a professional is acting merely as a businessman.

The patient as a consumer has major responsibilities to present the doctor/mental health professional with carefully written personal information, background details and a list of complaints, medications and if any, test results. This will not only allow the efficient use of time but also earn the professional's respect and desire to be actively involved.

Patients can also help themselves by utilizing the local library, the internet or by buying the relevant mental health books to educate themselves about their symptoms. They can also discuss the matter with their local doctor who may be sophisticated enough to offer professional guidance and refer them to the correct specialist. Of course goes without saying that all this requires openness, directness and not giving in to stigma or denials. Little risk taking can pay off in many ways, including saving money and distress.

Self-help therefore becomes essential not only to prevent crises but often to manage day-to-day life, relationships and working. Self-help solutions are plentiful in every culture. In the United States, there is even a National Mental Health Self-Help Clearinghouse that links individuals to self-help solutions. Almost all developed countries have professional associations, organizations, and societies that are more than willing to provide initial guidance and referrals. Often there are foundations specializing in different disorders such as depression, bipolar, and schizophrenia that are able to provide handouts, fliers, and other information. There is even an Alliance for Mentally Ill (NAMI) in the U.S., which does a great service by providing self-help resources to patients and their families. Developing countries still lack these resources and systems.

There are sections in bookstores stacked with books that offer solutions to specific problems. These books address common problems under specific topics such as alcoholism, depression, low self-esteem, stress management, anger management, how to have a happy marriage, parenting, assertiveness, dependency, understanding obsession-compulsions, managing anxiety and fears, etc.

There are professionals and organizations which sell self-help and motivational tools in the form of CDs, DVDs or mp3s. In many cities, Yoga classes and similar groups are commonplace nowadays, and these are a powerful tool for stress prevention and management.

There are support groups for people with conditions that range from migraine to menopause, bipolar disorder to baldness, alcoholism to fear of public speaking. Unlike Alcoholics Anonymous or its offspring, where the emphasis is on surrendering to the group philosophy, the focus of many of these tools or processes is self-direction. When they succeed, it is because they offer replicable structures, routines, and value systems that match user's needs. When they do not succeed, it may be because they have limited utility or relevance for those who have serious emotional disorders like psychosis, manic-depressive illness, personality disorders and may be in need of formal and sustained, professional treatment.

There are also ongoing workshops/seminar/conferences conducted in colleges, universities, hospitals and large cities on mental health topics

How to Self-Help

As mentioned earlier, the role of the individual in self-help is crucial – not only to prevent becoming a mental health consumer but, above all, to sustain wholesome living, harmonious relationships and feeling productive and happy. Most Indians usually grow up with good mental hygiene, clear values and basic skills for living life in a "straight line". For example, early to rise and early to bed, morning hygiene rituals, simple life style and routines, acceptance of life as it is, contentment, intimacy and respect for elders and others, surrendering feelings to assigned and expected roles and responsibilities, postponing individuality to nurture the larger family, tolerating extended family dictated choices of life style, foods and routines, etc. Straight line living is one of the major prophylactics for mental health i.e. following a culturally prescribed order of things: first education, then working, followed by marriage, having children followed by going on their own. In the western context, the intense preoccupation with individuality and autonomy often sabotages the completion of education, combining resources with the parents and siblings, sometime having children before marriage and establishing own households on borrowed money.

In the American context, the rushed autonomy leads to costly trial and error risking drug use, single motherhood, and living on borrowed money.

Indian culture, at its core, is parasympathetic nervous system oriented i.e. opposite of sympathetic orientation which triggers negative feelings, stress reaction and risk of dependence on tranquilizers, alcohol, food, commercial entertainment, and consumerism. In essence, external means to feel good, sustain self-esteem via an obsessive need to control.

In essence, Indians can cultivate and strengthen their emotional immunity by learning and practicing the healthy aspects of their value system, life style and culture as it has a built in defense against stress, doom gloom thinking, and panicking under adversity.

One has to be creative in terms of self-help options based on one's personal, cultural, religious and social realities. The following is a brief list of examples of self-help strategies:

Samkalpa. *A samkalpa* is a resolve (determined decision). It is an affirmation that is made to overcome any weakness affecting the body, performance, and life. It aims at awakening mind's strength to reclaim internal balance. These can be short sentences, vows, mantras that one can use to program the s mind in a particular positive direction. *Samkalpa*'s can be stated before a particular practice (such as yoga), during weakness or illness, or throughout the day. Regular practice can help focus, seek direction, fend off distractions, and enhance precise action.

Internal Chaos or loss of homeostasis arises from ignorance, which is rooted in responding based on likes and dislikes. A neutral mind produces harmony inside and outside.

Fasting. It's a powerful means to quieten the mind. It is not about giving up consumption but more about taking charge of reincarnating your karma and behavioral patterns. To fast is to give the mind and body a break from thinking, feeling and compulsion related overload. Obsessive consumption or habitual sensory interaction with food is not only disruptive and stressful, but also potentially addictive. If the mind is on the food, all other higher cognitive functioning usually stops. Absence of such stimuli can result in boredom, irrational acting out, or simply withdrawal. Fasting can reset the cognitive-emotional circuits and help the body and mind decrease its dependence on stimuli. This can be verbal fasting, involving the practice of silence and avoiding stimuli such as television, texting phone interaction; or physical fasting i.e. refraining from eating. Individuals suffering from serious illness such as diabetes and high blood pressure should consult their physician before practicing physical fasting. Inexperienced individuals should first practice skipping one or two meals, caffeine, sugar, grains, etc. before attempting full-fledged fasting.

Relaxation. Relaxation is in juxtaposition to stress which can be emotional, cognitive or physical. It's all in thinking and perceptions. Correct and scientific thinking and objective perceptions are best defense against and distress. Some stress is human and inevitable e.g. if you have an important appointment and you have a flat tire,

To manage one's sympathetic nervous system arousal, sensory excitement, and emotional overload, one needs to practice relaxation. Relaxation can be acquired by being quiet, simplifying thinking, focusing on breathing, simplifying thinking, meditation, praying, playing, worshipping or withdrawing. However, resorting to food, alcohol, smoking, drug, prescriptions or sex as a means to relax is risky, potentially harmful and counterproductive. One can develop addiction, have an injury or accident, get into legal trouble, and develop physical illness or end up wasting hard earned money.

Cognitive Restructuring. An undisciplined mind, if not managed, can wreak havoc on thoughts, feelings behavior, relationships or employment. We think in terms of words, language, images and conditioning – which determine our moods, anticipations, expectations and even our physical health. Healthier and spiritual belief system can efficiently stop the chattering of the mind and irrational thinking.

> *"The man who can see all creatures in himself, himself in all creatures, realizes oneness."*
>
> *- Ishopanishad*
>
> *"The good man has nothing to be anxious about, except what arises from his own folly"*
>
> *- Earnest Wood*

Living in the Moment. It is a common saying that the past is gone, the future is not yet here and therefore the present is the essence. The tendency of the mind is to think, imagine, jump from thought to thought, and react to every stimuli. It feels regrets and guilt about the past and catastrophizes about the future. Mind never stops. What it was, where one has been is a good therapeutic exercise but futile as to where one is and what one is becoming? Everything happens in the context of time. It is crucial to be able to relinquish preoccupation with the past and control projections about the future by simply surrendering and being in the moment. Breathing exercises and meditation are the most powerful techniques that can help one live in the moment

Practicing Rituals. Observing *Dharmic* rituals, such as participating in pilgrimages, community celebrations, *pooja*, and attending satsang can be very therapeutic as they evoke a relaxation response. One can also invent one's own rituals to neutralize stress. People in Western countries use "Happy Hour" as a time to let go of stress, but of course this revolves around alcohol. There is no reason one can't create one's own "Happy Hour" ritual that does not involve alcohol, sitting in smoky bars, listening to invasive, loud noises. A good example of happy hour could be "satsang", listening to soothing music, nature walks, therapeutic films, etc.

Self-Help Aphorisms

- *There is no perpetual happiness. Stress, pain, suffering, hurt, and let downs are waiting just around the corner.*

- *Death is inevitable and so is aging. Fear of death, uncertainty, and not knowing causes panic in most people.*

- *Relationships are never perpetually peaceful. One cannot live with them or without them.*

- *Free will is an illusion since responsibilities, obligations, the needs of significant others, and social interactions entangle us in the roller coaster, i.e. business of living day-to-day.*

- *Life is risky and it does not come with a fail-proof warranty.*

- *It is an unmistakable fact that every action has a consequence.*

- *One can plan but what really happens is an entirely different matter. One still has to act as if one is in charge and has a destination.*

Reading. The study of good books such as Bhagavad Gita has therapeutic value. Poetry reading is also known to be very useful. The author maintains a file titled "inspirational wisdom" for personal therapy.

Journal writing. One always needs to ask and answer *what is the purpose of life? Why one is here?* Journal writing is a versatile tool to get insight into oneself and to take emotional inventory of conflicts, weaknesses and strengths. Journal writing offers an opportunity to track one's priorities, personal growth as well as develop strategies to solve problems. In essence, one needs self-reorientation often and journal writing is a powerful option.

Inward Withdrawal. Sensory retraction is a powerful method to dissipate frustrations, anxiety, fear, and anger. It requires suspension of judgmental thinking, personalizing, stepping out of power struggles, having zero expectations and, in essence, identifying with nothing else, not even one's mind or body but only breathing. One can schedule brief sessions for oneself to go into inward withdrawal on a need or routine basis.

Learn Something New. Learning a new language, acquiring a hobby, taking up a cause, getting out of one's self by serving others, volunteering to care for unfortunate segments of the society, etc. promote sublimation i.e. redirection of energies into constructive directions. Stepping out of over-involvement with the material world, self-importance and narcissistic thinking is powerful therapy.

Make Decisions. Lots of emotional and interpersonal suffering, wavering, panicking, fearing, worrying, obsessing, anhedonia, regretting, dueling in doom gloom and failing to experience intimacy are rooted in confusions, ambivalences, self-created dilemmas, indecisiveness, compulsion to accumulate material possessions, ignorance based immaturities and prolonging living in a non-committal mindset. There is no substitute for making decisions e.g. after having acquired reasonable financial security, one needs to relinquish a money hoarding obsession. Similarly, when children become of age, it's essential to let go of micromanaging and worrying.

Stop Consumerism. In a capitalistic society, everything is packaged to sell and an army of salesmen earn their living by convincing public why it's essential for their happiness. Reality is just the other way around. One needs minimal to have a simple, peaceful and happy life. Commercial culture, even in the field of the mental health industry, has been releasing new books every few years, based on subjects from self-esteem, assertiveness, stress management, anger management, mindfulness, meditation, men are from mars, I am Ok, and you are Ok and . . . the list is endless. For sanity's sake, one does not need to be impacted by new catch phrases, chase every new gimmick and become dependent for feeling good on every new form of capitalistic Guru. Their strategy is first to point out you are damaged goods and then to request that you buy what they are selling and that, as a result, you will be happy ever after. The reality is that if you live simply, practice a healthy life style, go inward, follow wholesome *ashtang sankhya-yoga*, be genuinely spiritual and follow commonsense, then good self-esteem and happiness will follow. Of course, life will challenge you in the areas of health, work, marriage, parenting and relationships and for that you may have seek treatment from the specialists.

Treatment Considerations

Treatment for mental health issues, unlike physical health, is slighly challenging since public education is still limited. Moreover, the number, avialibity and the visibility of mental health professionals is somewhat limited. The stigma of seeking mental health services does not make it easy, either. Moreover, most patients needing help end up in emergency rooms, consulting the local doctor/vaidya/hakim or family punditji, none of which are usually efficient options. A great number of people also prefer to trust their family Guru, familiar Swamiji or some charlaton who practices witchcraft. None of these options are any good as they delay the treatment and promote exploiitation. Going from mandir to majare-sherif, ashrams to self proclaimed unqualified therapists is equally wasteful.

Mental health treatment is a science and there are no available short cuts or magic. There is no substitute for educating oneself via any available means and then seeking formal consultation/input from a professional.

Even if you know that you need more than a self-help solution, where do you start? How does one distinguish between types of therapists? How can you find a culturally competent therapist? What approach should one take when one is in crisis?

Let's approach these questions one-by-one.

Mental health professionals, in spite of their diversity in orientation and training, work collaboratively and in essence as a team. Even if a professional is from a different race, culture or religious background, he will be able to offer the diagnosis, necessary referral and even treatment. One does not need to be overly concerned about having to seek out a mental health professional at the initial stage of crisis. Once the crisis is resolved, one can share one's preference for mental health professional with compatible culture, religion or gender. Treating professionals will be very willing to help you find one.

Types of Therapists: There are basically four types: psychiatrists, psychologists, social workers and counselors.

Psychiatrists, due to their training and medical orientation, see mental problems as disorders of brain chemistry or some physical etiology and treat by prescribing medicines. At times, difficult problems may require Electric Shock Therapy as a last resort. Psychiatrists are able to admit and discharge patients in and out of crisis centers and hospitals.

Sometimes, the patient has to be treated in patient/hospital for the safety of self and others. Psychiatrists play a very important role since they are often the first to come in contact with the patient. This is slowly changing and psychologists are starting to become affiliated with the hospitals and may also have admitting and discharging privileges. In some places, they are also being considered for prescription privileges.

Culture tends to offer a cumulative wisdom to facilitate successfully and deal with one's psycho-socio-polico-spiritual context. However, cultures too can become confusing and sometimes contaminated due to historical influences and political movements often needing reforms, self-examination, and deceive remedies such as dowry and caste system etc. among Hindus. Mental health professionals (not religious authorities) have the primary obligation to tease out the therapeutic versus pathological aspects of the culture. They cannot be relevant to the patient, unless they are able to identify the individual's cultural context, concepts, definitions, ideals, and conflict dynamics. For example, Indian husbands often feel sandwiched between the competing demands of their parents and spouses. Muslim patients by and large terminate therapy after single session as they feel an overwhelming sense of being disloyal to their faith and family. In other words, every culture defines individuals' personal boundaries, values, and life destinations.

Psychologists, on the other hand, tend to define emotional problems more in terms of conflict with feelings, distorted thinking, confusions, negative habits, self-destructive life style, lacking behavioral, interpersonal, and decision-making skills. Their treatment orientation tends to be focused on teaching, coaching, modeling, talking, guiding, and promoting awareness of the patient's dysfunctional behavioral, cognitive, and emotional, interpersonal patterns. Psychologists accomplish their goals by utilizing verbal interaction, imagery, role-playing, behavioral management, modifications, hypnosis, cognitive-behavioral techniques, etc. to alter the patient's behavior. It is crucial to know that the psychologist's ultimate goal for the patient is to become self-dependent and not to need treatment as soon as possible.

Psychologists utilize numerous strategies to treat different conditions. A well-trained or experienced psychologist will take responsibility to refer the patient for psychiatric, neurological primary care provider (PCP), endocrinology, cardiology, pulmonology or other specialists to ensure that patients get the most comprehensive and effective treatment. A good psychologist, like a good Primary Care Physician, is the first line of defense. He can act as a gatekeeper and coordinate the entire treatment process

Social workers place greater emphasis on the role of social factors such as family systems, work context, socio-economic variables, relationships, etc. in determining the dysfunction. They actively involve family, significant others, and employer, etc. Social workers obtain detailed information as to the patient's living conditions, financial status before developing interventions. Licensed Clinical Social Workers are trained in psychotherapy and in working with social agencies to support the client's mental and physical well-being. Social workers cannot administer or interpret psychological testing, nor can they prescribe medication.

Licensed Professional Counselors are trained in general psychotherapy and assisting clients with various life problems (e.g., relationships, career, and overall well-being). Licensed counselors can provide some evaluation services, they are much more limited in scope compared to psychologist, social worker and psychiatrist.

Practitioner and the Cultural Implications

East is east and west is west, definitely applies to mental health. A person with a sense of self is uniquely a product of their culture. There are universal values which apply to all cultures but in therapy, the context is as to where the person is coming from and where he is going? In between all the other experiences which define personality for the individual are by product of Psycho-socio--econo-geo-political-religious background.

The context of Western therapy is rooted in euro-centric value system of "individualism", "person-centered", "existential perspective", hyper-focused on acquiring skills to be a successful consumer, "feelings first", practiced as a business, modeled after pure science and delivered in a framework of 'Therapist knows Best' framework and the consumer has to "fit in "via assimilation, acculturation" and learning western style skills and competencies of "separation, individuation, assertiveness, taking control and have a well-functioning executive ego to make it all happen seamlessly.

A holistic orientation is required to treat a person in order to address the mind and body aspects of the mental health consumer. Mind is a complex structure as it gives the individual a required unique identity. Physical characteristics are only an external and somewhat superficial introduction of a person. It's the mind maze that presents the challenge to the individual internally and to the mental health professional clinically. Mind is just not a storage of all the past experiences, images and memories but above all convergence of where the person has been, where he is coming from, what personal, familial, socio-economic, cultural, political, philosophical, religious and educational variables are defining him. Patient's values, beliefs, perceptions are a unique composite giving him a personality of his own. They are at the root of how a person sees self, others and the world. The entire journey of life is basically an unfolding of the unconscious (samskaras) as well as the destination the person is aiming to arrive at.

In reality, it is the therapist's burden to educate self about the patient's thinking, feelings, culture and preparing to meet the patient on his psychological "turf". However, it should be noted that all therapists, regardless of race, religion, and ethnicity, in their value system, tend to be democratic, ethical, transparent and patient-s oriented. Following are highlights as to the strikingly different thinking-emotional-behavioral patterns rooted in the culture:

Indian sense of self revolves around the interdependence with significant others, taking responsibility for caring for the loved ones and respecting the elders.

Individuality is viewed as secondary to the moral, social, economic, obligations and cultural obligations and duties. Sacrificing for the parents, siblings and even to the peripheral members of the extended family is considered sacred.

Personal autonomy by separating from significant others/extended family is not an Indian cultural thing. On the contrary, remaining connected, interacting routinely, and having no boundaries is typical. Even after settling abroad, younger generation continues to engage in daily phone calls, sending money and guiding the family back home. Physical space is not allowed to create psychological space.

Loyalty to the family is of utmost importance. It is displayed via making sacrifices of the personal comfort, personal space, postponing own priorities, expecting spouse and children to carry on the tradition. Loyalty is one of the reason that parents will devastated with children's Americanization or family members accepting acculturation i.e. becoming absorbed or lost in mainstream/majority culture. I remember a friend who had been in the US for over 35 years and was successful in every way. He used to have a recurrent dream of swimming across the Atlantic Ocean to reach his home in Aligarh, UP.

Love for Indians is not a simple chemistry or one word thing. In Indian languages there are over 10 words to say "love" and it is defined differently to convey love towards god, mother/parents, children, lover, friends, spouse, etc. Moreover, Indians do not resort to verbal repetition of "I love you" nor they use cards, gifts, tokens or reassurances to convey the feeling. It is subtle and often is conveyed by behavior, tone of voice, gestures and personal sacrifices. Commercialized tokens such as cards, cakes, balloons, gifts or drama are considered as shallow and "cheapening" the whole notion of love.

Simplicity is the core of an Indian culture. It's often mistaken for miserliness, thriftiness or being cheap. Indians fear possessions as it offends their sense of modesty. Indian assume consumer role mostly when they "need" and not "want "something. Indian simplicity almost border on obsessiveness. However, it does not apply to earning, accumulating and multiplying and managing wealth due to historical insecurity rooted in colonial mindset.

Indian sense and sensibilities involving privacy, personal space and boundaries are absent to minimal. It is common to directly ask others for their age, income, nature of work, or even other personal details. etc. The filter is absent since culturally it is not seen as crude or significant.

Hierarchy and Indians are synonymous. Indians cannot relate to others without putting them into some or other category and label them as aunt, uncle, friend, etc. It is Indian way of defining their place in the packing order whether it's a family get together, party or a community function. The packing order typically revolves around age, caste, education, profession, personal accomplishments, and affiliation with Very Important people/celebrities/politicians/government officials, etc.

Indians cling to their traditions in spite of their worldly appearance and selective acculturation. Having a conservative household involves having a shrine, eating familiar food, carrying out various rituals like back home, etc. The parents' photos sit next to the Hindu gods and deities. They may be scientists or physicians but in their personal lives, they hang on to the traditions.

Feelings which form the core of western mind do not have an important place in the Indian culture. It is not that they are not recognized but basically they are dreaded due to their power of dictating one's behavior. Indian culture has developed and prescribed powerful mechanisms to suppress, repress, neutralize and manage them. Indians like control at mind level i.e. as a prophylactic to avoid behavioral complications. Feelings like desire are to be subordinated to thought and thought to "duty bound actions". This introduces rigidity in Indian behavior but it's culturally opted for.

The world has become small and, in many ways, the West and East are rapidly merging and fusing in somewhat complex ways. In the world of psychology and mental health, two developments have loosened the stranglehold of psychoanalytical and behaviorist approaches and shaped a Western openness to integrating the psychologies of the East. The 1960s and 1970s gave birth to the increasing popularity of meditation and Patanjali's Sankhya-Yoga in the West and a corresponding interest in the study of consciousness. At the same time, the emergence of transpersonal psychology also brought to focus the Indian psycho-spiritual and socio-philosophical traditions as valuable resources for understanding the nature of mind and consciousness.

Western practitioners have integrated rather well many of the clinical procedures from Vedanta and Buddhism. Ignorantly Buddhism is mistaken as separate & independent from Hinduism.

"The world is one family."

An Indian patient does understand how to be a good patient due to cultural pattern of displaying respect and obedience. He does not recognize the importance of being an equal partner in his own care. No matter how inconvenient, he relates like an obedient child with all prescribed dietary restrictions, medicine s or prescribed changes. But when it comes to emotional distress, the traditional Indian patient approaches his emotional distress via sharing with the nearest available elderly, wise man in the inner circle, family Guru, monk, pundit, or some other senior person. He is merely seeking direction, advice, words of wisdom, or reassurance that his problems are transient and there is no reason to feel despondent. Trusting is also built in since he is seeking the advice of older, experienced and mature person

However, an Indian patient more often than not is a challenge for the mental health professional. I remember a case of a young Indian Muslim boy who was asked by the school to seek help. After initial feedback, his family chose to change the school rather than to deal with the issues. The family could not conceive that they would be exposed to others. I know they would have even gone back to India rather than involving mental health, marital, or family counseling in the U.S.

As mentioned earlier, it is vital to understand that Indian families and marriages exist and function around a very delicate system based on hierarchy's faith, duties, traditions, rituals and understood but unspoken expectations. The protocols are complex but Indians grow up with them and usually follow them. . On the part of the therapist, any premature probing, attempt to introduce change, or identification of feelings can be overwhelming and destructive or at least debilitating. Indian families do not have contingency alternatives to their conflicts as they never expect or anticipate infidelity, drug use, marital breakdown, pregnancies before or outside marriage, etc. Separations, Divorces, single motherhood, etc. are not yet adequately familiar. They are more familiar and much better prepared as to survival in case of spouse's death, significant others being away for long periods for work or military duty or daughter in law's demanding separate household. Indians also lack contingency plans on how to care for children in the case of divorce. This is one of the reasons that Indian spouses linger on even if the marriage is miserable or act out dangerously. The contingency mind set tends to be absent. The premise is all or nothing.

The reader must keep in mind that the similar observations will not apply to the same extent to an Indian client who has been living in the West and certainly not to the one who has been born and brought up in the USA, Canada, or in the UK. This is for the simple reason that they are exposed to counselors and mental health professionals early on either in the school or through TV, movies, newspaper articles, etc.

However, the older generation remains heavily influenced by the traditions, cultural prescripts and historical legacies. The differences are pervasive and apply not only as to the perception of the mental health service provider, but also how to hand over personal information, deal with feelings, or talk to an outsider about private family matters. The older generation also feels that their distress is merely a consequence of their own deeds or karma, and have to be lived through, and not escaped. This deeply held value system of acceptance and resignation are also major barriers toward convincing the patient that change is possible, and that taking control of one's feelings and what happens to them in life is manageable and can be improved. Conveying hope for the unfamiliar is frightening.

Indian self-help rituals are also considered to be important adjuncts to seeking professional help. For example, fasting, religious rituals, and varieties of self-sacrifices are often utilized to cope with or stop the suffering. I knew a mother who had taken vows never to eat eggplants following her son's illness and she never did. In addition, Indian Ayurvedic dietary practice holds that changing what one eats can cure the ills of the body-mind. Different foods are categorized in terms of their properties of Vata, Pitta, Kaffa and certain combinations are prohibited due to their ill effect on the body. For example, one is not supposed to drink water after eating peanuts. Similarly, one is prohibited from eating sour foods or beverages if one is coughing or has a sore throat. Fasting is practiced if one is suffering from fever. The very first step an Indian takes, when feeling ill, is to reduce or stop the consumption of salt, oil, khatai and chilies to bring the body back to balance. In olden days and even currently at the village level, certain abnormal behaviors are dealt with through purification rituals and shamanic approaches. The belief here is that the individual is under the control of some evil spirit. The "evil eye" may also be viewed as a cause of mental disorder or physical distress. The context behind such a naïve view is that daily life is so simple, basic, routine, and predictable that one rarely sees an episode of mental disorder. Therefore when a disorder occurs, the etiology is seen as coming from outside the person. However, this perspective is changing rather rapidly as alcoholism, manic depressive episodes, depression, suicides, and homicides are on the rise.

Initiating Therapeutic Alliance.

As a mental health professional, you have only one chance to make it all work from generating trust, earning respect to developing an alliance for compliance. First impressions really matter in particular when a patient is coming from a cultural background where it is uncommon to seek *mental health help or expose very personal, marital, parental or and family details. In the Indian mind, it's crossing the boundaries of sacredly held loyalties. Additionally,* patient may be afraid that by indulgence in examining the issues, it may become worse and out of control. Some reassurance and conveying optimism will be required on the part of the therapist.

As to initiating actual psycho-therapy/psychiatric treatment, the initial contact sets the pace of the progress and outcome. It is conceivable that the patient is not interested in consulting and in all likelihood in an ongoing treatment. In particular, he may not believe that talk therapy is useful. He has the mindset that even one consultation is a waste of time, and may present the façade of being courteous, pleasant, and even cooperative while underneath eager to get out of therapist's office as soon as possible. He may believe there is a better use of the money and time, and may only be coming because of some external mandate, such as pressure from her employer, a court order, or a threat of divorce. Indian patient tend to reach out only when he is desperate and no other option is left.

Hindus tend to see loss of emotional balance even physical problems as a result of personal failure or at best result of bad karma. Emotional Imbalance is interpreted in terms of either lack of self-discipline or bad habits, As a result, the therapist needs to be sensitive to patient's cultural value system to facilitate trusting and engagement in the treatment process. It is counterproductive to rush to introduce the mental health terms or diagnosis etc. It will only overwhelm the patient and may result in noncompliance. Patient should be tolerated as to his catharsis or rambling involving his "pity party" feeling helpless and blaming everything from bad karma to everybody else in the world. Therapist has to wait for an opening to change the direction toward the therapeutic alliance. Often such openings evolve when the patient becomes aware that his best, most productive and cost effective option is psycho-therapy and/or psychiatric medicine.

One can imagine as to what concerns, anxiety, reservations and confused expectations the person may be bringing with him. These apprehensions often cause the patient not to keep the appointment, cancel at the last minute or come late. Another response is to arbitrarily change the ground rules and expect to have the session on the phone. I have also seen instances in which the patient does not get the clues to end the session and instead engage in prolonging it. This does not happen because the patient has a rapport with you but only because he is paying and wants to maximize his return.

Some of these issues can be better handled by first focusing on non-clinical matters, i.e., telling the patient that you are extremely busy and successful and that without him becoming your patient, you will still be fine. In other words, you do not need his business. This may seem rather crude, but I have often used it immediately to settle a patient's fantasy that all you care about is collecting your fee.

I also ask all my patients if they have any fee limitations and if they want to discuss needing some exceptions. I make it very clear that in future all money transactions will be handled by the secretary, including phone contacts and scheduling appointments. Of course, this is unnecessary if the patient is sophisticated.

If she is not, it saves lot of frustrations later to explain at the outset the culture of your practice, your value system about money, and the importance of mutual punctuality. Indian patients respond better if the professional rather than the office staff carries out the initial pre-session contact. The focus of the pre-session should be mutual introduction, explanation of psychotherapy and how it works, what the patient can expect, and office policies regarding short notice cancellations, fees, payment methods, etc. It will also help to mail the patient a letter with an appointment card and clear directions to avoid last minute frenzied calls that he is lost or how to get to the office.

Some additional considerations:

- Provide structure to listen, but also to clarify concepts such as setting professional boundaries, and to spell out what you as a professional will and will not do. It should be made very clear that you will not discuss payment and appointment issues again and again It should also be spelled out that you do not want to be called at odd hours or contacted at home, nor should you permit the patient to bypass office staff for scheduling appointments. Training the patient to honor boundaries is the first step to structuring therapy.

- Sometimes psychological testing may be necessary, as well as referring the patient for a second opinion, either to establish diagnosis, rule out some other specific disease or to manage the illness. The patient deserves to have information explained and to be gently prepared.

The patient's expectations must be clarified to remove any confusion, discrepancies or misunderstanding. It should be conveyed that there are no short cuts and that the entire process is carried out legitimately in accordance with the professional ethics, insurance rules, and within the prescribed norms. You may encounter patients who pursue short cuts in place of therapy. An example is a patient who once offered me a bribe to write him a letter saying that he was not an alcoholic and that he had completed his treatment for DUI.

Handling the Preliminaries

The need to take care of the mechanics and to remove any emotions from the process cannot be overemphasized. In my office, we negotiate this aspect three times: on the phone before the actual appointment, via a follow-up signed contract after the phone appointment, and at the beginning of the first session. Taking the time to get clarity on these issues will allow the clinical focus to go uninterrupted without any unnecessary games, such as the patient trying to renegotiate fees. If feasible, the clinician should in this first phase give the patient some idea as to approximately how many sessions will be essential. Because only short-term therapy is acceptable to many Indian clients, even the very first session should be approached as total therapy from diagnosis to feedback. In that case, the patient has all necessary information even if he does not return. I always encourage my patients to find a practitioner that is near their home or more convenient than I as to distance. I have found that the best way to cure for the Empire State Building-size Indian ego is deflate it very early by conveying you are happy to help them find someone else.

Overview of the Treatment Process

Each patient is unique and requires individualized treatment planning. Once the patient is educated about the process, the clinician can concentrate on diagnosis and treatment. Treatment cannot be initiated unless the mechanics of appointments, authorizations and permissions, payment options are worked out thoroughly. Many tasks are carried out by the office staff. This can be accomplished by patient coming few minutes earlier than his appointment. Patient should come with a copy and information of all of his record of health, treatment, medicine, test results as well as information about his person and background. Often it's also useful to have the family members available for an initial appointment. This will save time, money and help the professional to see a complete picture. Additionally, it will ensure safety of the patient if in case the patient is experiencing paranoia, agitation, mania or suicidal ideation.

I recommend a three-phase approach with mental health clients. In each of these phases, avoid a process-oriented approach in favor of a more directed one, using behavioral prescriptions. Teaching, modeling, and providing task assignments work much better than sharing and processing feelings. Although Indian patients' built-in obsessive compulsively can seem like a barrier to growth, it is paradoxically also an asset and can be utilized to effectively engage the patient in accomplishing certain tasks. For example, the assignment of specific readings, or watching a particular movie, can be excellent tools to clarify certain concepts or teach skills.

First Phase: During the initial diagnostic interview and observation, help the patient conduct an inventory of her strengths and weaknesses as a means of uncovering the pattern that is tied to the problematic behavior. At the same time, highlight her character strengths and how she can utilize them to solve domestic problems, achieve success at work, speed up adjustment, or enhance security. This is not always easy, as I have had many patients who were highly educated and professionally successful but were unable to relate their feelings to their behavior or understand the concept of introspection. It is also difficult for some patients to see the impact of their behavior on others (significant or outsiders) or have awareness as to how others feel.

For example, a software engineer I worked with after several sessions was still not fully convinced that the simple act of occasionally bringing home a red rose for his wife would make her feel special. His wife had clearly asked for this gesture, as he was routinely giving flowers to her aunt. His wife wanted so little to feel acknowledged by her husband. He kept telling me that his wife was the most important person in his life and he believed that thinking it was sufficient. In other words, he lacked empathy due to his emotional immaturity and lack of empathy for wife's feelings.

Middle Phase: During this phase, highlight and educate the patient about the diagnosis, and provide written information describing it but without terrifying the patient. No matter what take an optimistic approach, Point out the risks and consequences if the condition is untreated, i.e., the impact of the symptoms and unresolved problems on the family, finances, and future. You can also ask the patient to do some homework and to elf educate about their illness. Recommend reading of specific books or watching movies to should be prescribed to facilitate understanding. I routinely advise that alcoholic patients read the "Big Book" published by Alcoholic Anonymous. With the popularity of Internet the task of finding relevant material almost on any topic has become very easy.

The patient usually needs help with neutralizing negative feelings (anger, fear, sadness, anxiety helplessness, worrying, guilt, shame, failure, unworthiness, split between conflicting roles and obligations). Such distress typically is rooted in, often, incompatible demands of being in multiple roles, such as husband, parent, child, and sibling. Unlike in the Western culture, an Indian continues to feel responsible as well as obligated to carry out his expected roles without any modification, as the life progresses. Sometimes these responsibilities are externally imposed and obligatory, but most often they are self-imposed to help the patient feel good about herself and gain acceptance from others – a costly way to prove one's loyalty to the family.

Often, negative feelings are connected to unmet expectations. For example, sons, daughters, or daughters-in-law may feel let down by significant others and as a result are unable to sustain respect for those who have not met their expectations. They may feel guilt and anguish about their lack of respect, which may result in depression, rage or acting out. Until recently, Indians did not externalize these symptoms and primarily reacted to them solely on the thinking level. However, this is changing and Indians are becoming more emotionally expressive in their reactions.

Final Phase: As the risk of abrupt termination, noncompliance or no-shows is very high, it is very important to educate the patient about the process of therapy termination very early on. He should be assisted and encouraged to make a specific, simple, and relevant list of post-treatment goals. If he is receptive, monthly follow-up sessions can be scheduled. Clearly emphasize the need for follow-up, whether this involves meeting with other physicians, taking medication, life style changes, or engaging in self-help solutions. Before termination, ideally, family should be explained their role for support and understanding.

Current Status of Mental Health Services

The main obstacle to widespread mental health treatment throughout the world is *access*. The supply of mental health professionals is meager to absent in most places. Seeing a therapist or a psychiatrist in the developed world is costly, and an ongoing care can turn into a financial hardship. Most people really cannot afford unless they have health insurance. Even health insurances may have hefty copayments.

In reality, Psychiatrists are too busy to spare more than a few minutes with a patient. Psychologists do not prescribe medicine and therapy sessions are limited to 45 minutes at best. Most social workers work for agencies rather than in practice. However, it is improving. Social workers limitations is not only that they do not prescribe, cannot administer psychological tests but often do not have access to see patients in the hospitals. Many Social workers counselors and therapists can be very competent, versatile, and good gatekeepers to facilitate patient's care.

In the developing world, mental health remains neglected and mental health professionals are available only in big cities. The culture and the business mindset of the mental professionals is pathetic as they avoid team approach and the status based hierarchy obstructs communication among professionals. They lack sophistication and the compassion to educate the patient about medicine side effects, inform the patient as to the diagnosis and spell out the course of the treatment. Every time patient has a side effect, feeling better, feeling overwhelmed, patient has to schedule an appointment, pay hefty fee and travel long distances under adversarial traffic situations. The politics of the economics of the mental health favors only mental health professionals and not the consumer. Government run hospitals do not offer mental health services. Charitable organizations also have not yet included mental health care. In essence, the situation is very gloomy while mental health needs are of epidemic proportion. The trend is that mental health crisis will continue to grow sabotaging individuals, marriage, families and the national productivity.

Psychiatric Medications

Psychotropic (psychiatric/mental medications) drugs play an important role in managing the crisis, treating serious disorders and often as a concurrent treatment with psychological treatment. Herbs, vitamins, *Ayurvedic* drugs or self-medication via street drugs are not good options when one has mental disorders. Initially, psychiatrist may need to see patient weekly, for about 6-8 weeks, to make sure that right medication has been prescribed and that there are no significant side effects. Often more than one medication is prescribed until the psychiatrist feels sure what is least essential and the best medication. Some medications need blood work to determine the level of efficacy and to avoid toxicity. This can be expensive. So, patient should discuss with the doctor to get cheaper or free medications.

Warnings as to the Medications and more:

- Medications are not substitutes for good psychotherapy, improving life style and self-help or vice versa. Informed and educated patient is a better consumer. Never to alter medications without first letting the physician know. If not accessible personally, make phone call, send a text, an email, or letter.
- In case of severe side effects, stop or reduce the dosage or number of medications and immediately make an appointment to see the doctor. A local pharmacist can also be of some assistance.
- Patient should be educated as to what medications are addictive or what side effects are possible. Encourage them to contact their pharmacy or the doctor immediately if they experience out-of-the-ordinary symptoms.

Consumers must be informed about types of drugs and their effects. Here is a brief list of commonly prescribed medicines. Since brand names differ from country to country, it is important to know the generic names of the drugs.

- Anti-anxiety/Anxiolytic (addictive): Xanax, Valium, Librium, Klonopin, Ativan, Serex, Tranxene, Atarax, Buspar, Benedryl, Inderal, Tenormin, Catapres, Restoril.
- Antidepressants (not addictive but risk if discontinued abruptly): Paxil, Prozac, Zoloft, Serzone, Effexor, Luvox, Wellbutrin, Desyrel, Sinequan, Elavil, Norpramin, Pamelor, Sinequan, Asendin, Celexa, Lexapro, Remeron, Vivectil, Eldepryl, Tofranil. Note: Some patients do not respond to this class of drugs and therefore ECT becomes a treatment of last resort. Suicidal patients especially should be hospitalized and closely monitored.
- Anti-Obsession/Compulsion: Selective serotonin re-uptake inhibitor (SSRIs) include Prozac, Zoloft, Paxil, Luvox, and Anafranil. Note: SSRIs are known to address symptoms of anxiety and depression. Sometimes, unpredictably, they may trigger a hypomania phase in a patient. There is no way to know in advance

since these same medications are successfully used for bipolar and manic depressive patients.

- *Psycho-stimulants* (used for ADD/ADHD kids): Adderall, Ritalin, Cylert, Dexedrine, Strattera, Concerta, Metadata.
- *Mood Stabilizers/Anticonvulsants* (used for Manic Depressive/Bipolar disorder): Depakote, Tegretol, Eskalith/Lithium, neurontin, Cerebyx, Lamictal, Trileptal, Topamax.
- Antipsychotic (schizophrenia, paranoia, schizoaffective, etc.): Risperdal, Haldol, Navane, Prolixin, Stelazine, Loxitane, Trilafon, Moban, Serentil, Clozaril, Mellaril, Thorazine, Abilify, Loxitane, Zyprexa, Geodon.
- *Anti-addiction:* Antabuse, Dolophin, Revex, Narcan, Buprenex.
- *MAO* inhibitors. *Note:* These are another set of medications which are utilized for OCD, and borderline personality disorders. They have to be watched very carefully as consumption of wine and cheese can be lethal while on these medications. Nardil, Parnate, Eldepryl/Carbex.

Many non-psychiatric medications may mimic or cause serious mental disorders such as depression, anxiety, and even psychosis. The list is long and one has to learn to take advantage of pharmacist for advice.

Elderly people have to be extra careful taking medications and they must consult a physician with gerontology expertise about dosages, etc.

Pregnant women and breast-feeding mothers must also seek expert advice due to risk of miscarriage, organicity, neonatal side effects like toxicity and withdrawal symptoms, long term neuro-behavioral effects, ADHD, Learning Disabilities, etc.

Similarly an expert must carefully evaluate the use of mental medications with children under six. In case of adolescents, the risk of overdose or suicide should also be monitored.

Alcohol, coffee, tea, tobacco masala, cigarettes act like medicines and can complicate the effects of medications. Avoid them totally. Maintaining a journal logging about medications, symptoms, mood and behavioral changes can be useful for the doctor and the patient alike.

Epilogue

- Mental health issues are merely indicative of our humanity. None of us are above being vulnerable or totally immune to feeling our feelings, thinking our thoughts, or ending up behaving in ways that are contrary to our belief system or the society's expectations. Individuals and society have always been engaged in a perpetual dance of approach-avoidance, complying-rebelling or seeking autonomy while society enforcing conformity and unconditional surrender.

- Common Religions of the world are the old-time philosophical psychologies emerged to help and manage individuals' vulnerabilities and social issues. They served well in the past. The reason they are becoming obsolete and less relevant in our present times, is only because they have a rigid belief that if one is good one will be happy. The reality is more complex and goodness does not guarantee happiness nor vice versa. Religions will continue to diminish in relevance because of their excessive use of fear, guilt, and hierarchy as controlling tools. Modern men and women are seeking autonomy and spirituality which is all inclusive and does not divide faithful vs. outsiders.

- Modern psychology's biggest contribution has been to point out that feelings are real, powerful, and always suppressing or repressing are not the only options. Hindu psychology's major contribution has been to offer highly sophisticated procedures to promote sublimation as a tool to manage feelings but also to integrate complex reality of feelings and psycho-socio-econo-spiritual dimensions. Hindu psychology prescriptions of four ashramas: *Brahmacharya*, *Grahastha*, *Vanaprastha*, and *Sanyasa*, practice of *Sankhya-Yoga*, techniques to manage desires, ego and attachment, etc. Psychology will continue to become increasingly more relevant and acquire the role of new religions. Psychology is better equipped to serve the globalized world where integration rather than division is important.

- Mental health professionals have a calling, beyond being entrepreneurs and specialists. Society needs adequate mental health services with choices from private practice, general hospitals, and outpatient programs to psychiatric institutions. The world is vast and no needy individual can be left behind. The issue is not always economic prosperity, technological and industrial success for a country to be proud of but services with easy access. People need to have access to diverse, affordable mental health services. Mental health professionals need to be transparent, spiritually oriented and inspired. Mental health services cannot operate by being devoid of spirituality. Spirituality being defined as spirit of oneness with all creation. If the goal is making big money then mental health professions are not the best options.

Each patient comes with a background of not only unique individuality but of religion, culture, family traditions, and the geo-political context. Mental health professionals and service providers will be ill equipped if lacked cross cultural sensitivity. The professional-patient matching requires appropriate training and availability of people with diverse languages, religions and subcultures. Such need can be met only if the planning is carried at a national and state level. Indian Diaspora is huge, scattered the world over, and there is an urgency that such services are made available. Many countries where diaspora resides have no mental health services. The stress and the strains of living in alien cultures, socio-economic-political hardships and religious-racial threats have depleted the Diaspora's resilience. The international Indian community can adopt the causes of the Diaspora as part of their Bhakti yoga, *vanaprastha* phase giving and opportunities for training for the younger generation. It may even generate employment opportunities. Jewish diaspora is a good model as it routinely promotions volunteering, resource sharing, networking and keeping diverse populations connected. Indian community centers and local organizations can assume responsibilities for specific projects i.e. preventing domestic violence, depression and suicides, alcoholism and drug addiction, intergenerational conflicts, marital and family breakdown, etc. Additionally, support for Indians in foreign prisons, exploited Indian workers in the Middle East, and victims of political upheavals are other areas where Diaspora needs services. Establishment of an India diaspora hot line with branches in every country for crisis intervention and referral will be a good place to start. Annual *Pravasi Bharatiya Divas* hosted in India can be used to encourage meetings and programs for the mental health professionals, volunteers and local leaders from different countries to initiate mental health service projects. Indian Diaspora has major weaknesses. It exists only at a local level in isolation. The information access is negligible. Leadership has to evolve to recognize the needs and challenges beyond economic survival. Community organizations must start the culture of offering crisis intervention, social support or provide guidance and referral.

Appendix A: List of Mental Disorders

The following list has been adapted from the ICD9, DSM IV R, and other sources

Disorders First Diagnosed by Age 18

- Mental Retardation; Mild, Moderate, Severe, Profound
- Learning Disorders; Reading, Mathematics, Written Expression
- Communication Disorders; Expressive Language, Mixed Receptive-Expressive, Phonological, Stuttering or Communication Disorder NOS
- Pervasive Developmental Disorder; Autistic, Rett's, Childhood Disintegrative, Asperger's or Pervasive Developmental Disorder NOS
- Attention Deficit & Disruptive Disorders; Attention-Deficit/Hyperactivity Disorder, Combined Type, Predominantly Inattentive Type, Predominantly Hyperactive-Impulsive Type, Attention Deficit/Hyperactivity Disorder NOS, Conduct Disorder, Oppositional Defiant Disorder or Disruptive Behavior Disorder
- Feeding & Eating Disorder of infancy/Early Childhood; Pica, Rumination Disorder, or Feeding Disorder
- Tic Disorders; Tourette's, Chronic Motor or Vocal Tic, Transient Tic or Tic Disorder
- Eliminations Disorder; Encoprosis, With constipation & Overflow, Without Constipation & Overflow or Enuresis (Non-Medical caused)
- Other Disorders of Infancy/Childhood/Adolescence; Separation Anxiety, Selective Mutism, Reactive Attachment, Stereotypic Movement or Not Otherwise Specified/NOS
- Delirium; Due to General Medical Condition, Substance Intoxication, Substance Withdrawal, Multiple Etiology, Delirium NOS Amnestic Disorders; Due to General Medical Condition/Substance-Induced Persisting or NOS
- Dementia; Alzheimer's Type (Uncomplicated/With Delusions/With Depressed Mood)
- Vascular Dementia; (Uncomplicated/With Delusions/With Depressed Mood)
- Dementia Due to Creutzfeldt-Jacob Disease
- Dementia Due to HIV Disease
- Dementia Due to Head Trauma

- Dementia Due to Huntington's Disease
- Dementia Due to Medical Condition
- Dementia Due to Multiple Etiologies or NOS
- Dementia Due to Parkinson's Disease
- Dementia Due to Pick's Disease
- Substance-Induced Persisting Dementia
- Other Cognitive Disorders
- Mental Disorders Due to a General Medical Condition; Catatonic, Personality Change Due to Medical Condition
- Substance-Related Disorders (Bhang, Tadee, Beer, Wine, Hard Liquor); Dependence on Alcohol or Abuse of Alcohol, Alcohol Withdrawal/Alcohol Intoxication Delirium/Alcohol Withdrawal Delirium/Alcohol-Induced Persisting Amnesic Disorder/Alcohol-Induced Psychotic Disorder (With Delusions/With Hallucinations, Alcohol-Induced Mood Disorder/Alcohol-Induced Anxiety Disorder/Alcohol-Induced Sexual Dysfunction/ Alcohol-Induced Sleep Disorder
- Amphetamine or Similar Drug Related Disorder (Speed, Uppers, Crank, Black Beauties, Crystal; Amphetamine Dependence/Abuse/Intoxication/Intoxication With Perceptual Disturbances/Withdrawal/Intoxication Delirium/Induced Psychotic Disorder (with Delusions/With hallucinations)/Induced Mood Disorder/Induced Anxiety Disorder/Induced Sexual Dysfunction / Induced Sleep Disorder/NOS
- Caffeine-Induced Disorders; Intoxication/Induced Anxiety Disorder/Induced Sleep Disorder or NOS
- Cannabis (dope, pot, grass, weed, herb, hash, joint) Related Disorders; Dependence/Abuse, Intoxication/ Intoxication With Perceptual Disturbances/Intoxication Delirium/Induced Psychotic Disorder (With Delusions/With Hallucinations), Induced Anxiety Disorder or NOS
- Cocaine Use Disorders (Coke, Rock, Crack, Base); Intoxication/Intoxication With Perceptual Disturbances, Withdrawal, Intoxication Delirium, Induced Psychotic Disorder I with delusions/With Hallucinations)/Induced mood disorder/Induced Anxiety Disorder/Induced Sexual Dysfunction/Induced Sleep Disorder or Induced Related NOS
- Hallucinogen Related Disorder; Dependence/Abuse, Persisting Perceptual Disorder/NOS
- Inhalant Related Disorders (gas, aerosols, glue, nitrites, rush, whiteout); Dependence/Abuse, Intoxication/ Intoxication /Intoxication Delirium, Induced Persisting Dementia/Induced

Psychotic Disorder (With Delusions/With Hallucinations)/Induced Mood Disorder/Induced Anxiety Disorder or NOS
- Nicotine Related Disorder; Dependence, Withdrawal or NOS
- Opioid Use Disorders (Heroin, Morphine, Codeine, Delaudid, Demerol, Black Tar, China White); Dependence/Abuse, Intoxication, Intoxication with Perceptual Disturbances, Withdrawal, Intoxication Delirium, Induced Psychotic Disorder (With Delusions/With Hallucinations), Induced Mood Disorder. Induced Sexual Dysfunction, Induced Sleep Disorder or NOS
- Phencyclidine/Like Related Disorder; Dependence/abuse, Intoxication, Intoxication With Perceptual Disturbances, Intoxication Delirium, Induced Psychotic Disorder (With Delusions/With hallucinations), Induced Mood Disorder, Induced Anxiety Disorder or NOS
- Sedative, Hypnotic, Or Anxiolytic Related Disorder (Kava Kava, Barbiturates, downers, tranquilizers, ludes, reds, valium, Xanax; Dependence/Abuse, Intoxication, Withdrawal, Intoxication Delirium, Induced Persisting Dementia, Induced Persisting Amnestic Disorder, Induced Psychotic Disorder (With Delusions/With Hallucinations), Induced Mood Disorder/Induced Anxiety Disorder, Induced Sexual Dysfunction, Induced Sleep Disorder or NOS
- Poly-substance i.e. simultaneous use of many drugs abuse Related Disorder
- Psychotic Disorders such as Schizophrenia ; Paranoid Type, Disorganized Type, Catatonic Type, Undifferentiated Type, or Residual Type
- Schizophreniform Disorder
- Schizoaffective Disorder (psychosis + mood disorder combined); Bipolar Type, Depressive Type
- Delusional Disorder (cognitive distortions)
- Psychotic Disorder Due to General Medical Condition (With Delusions &/or With Hallucinations)
- Brief Psychotic Disorder (With or Without Marked Stressor)
- Shared Psychotic Disorder
- Substance (alcohol or drugs, prescribed or illegal) Induced Psychotic Disorders
- Psychotic Disorder NOS
- Mood Disorders
- Major Depression (Single Episode/Recurrent)
- Dysthymic Disorder (garden variety depression due to loss or disappointments)

- Depressive Disorder NOS
- Bipolar/Manic Depressive Disorders
- Bipolar I (Single Manic Episode/Mixed, Most Recent Episode Hypomanic/ Most Recent Episode Manic/Most Recent Episode Mixed/Most Recent Episode Depressed/Most Recent Episode Unspecified
- Bipolar Disorder II
- Cyclothymic Disorder
- Bipolar Disorder NOS
- Mood Disorder Due to General Medical Condition. (With Depressive Features/ With Major Depression Episode/With Manic Features/With Mixed Features)
- Substance Induced Mood Disorder
- Mood Disorder NOS
- Anxiety Disorders (Panic & with or Without Agoraphobia)
- Agoraphobia with or without History of Panic Disorder
- Specific Phobias (Animal Type/Natural Environment Type/Blood-Injection-Injury Type/Situational Type/Other Type)
- Social Phobia
- Obsessive-Compulsive Disorder (OCD)
- Post-traumatic stress disorder (Acute/Chronic/ With Delayed Onset)
- Acute Stress Disorder
- Generalized Anxiety Disorder (GAD/Worrying/ chinta)
- Anxiety Due to Generalized Medical Condition (With Panic Attacks/With Obsessive Compulsive Symptoms)
- Substance Induced Anxiety Disorder
- Anxiety Disorder NOS
- Somatoform Disorder (Somatization/Undifferentiated. Somatoform/Conversion With Motor Symptom/Or Deficit/With Seizures or Convulsions/With Sensory Symptom/Deficit/With Mixed Presentation)
- Pain Disorder (Associated With Psychological Factors/Both With Psychological Factors & a General Medical Condition)
- Hypochondriasis (With Poor Insight)
- Body Dysmorphic Disorder
- Somatoform Disorder NOS
- Factitious Disorders (With Predominantly Psychological Signs& Symptoms/Physical Signs & Symptoms/combined Signs & Symptoms or NOS)
- Dissociative Disorders (Dissociative Amnesia/Fugue)

- Dissociative Identity Disorder
- Depersonalization Disorder
- Dissociative Disorder NOS
- Sexual & Gender Identity Disorder
- Sexual Dysfunctions; Lifelong Type/Acquired Type/Generalized Type/Situational Type/Due to Psychological Factors
- Sexual Desire Disorders; Hypoactive/Aversion
- Sexual Arousal Disorders; (Female Arousal/Male Erectile Disorder)
- Orgasmic Disorders; Female Orgasmic/Male Orgasmic/Premature Sexual Pain Disorders; Dyspareunia /Vaginusmus (Not Due to General Medical Condition)
- Sexual Dysfunction Due to a General Medical Condition; Female Hypoactive Sexual Desire/Male Hypoactive Sexual Desire/Male Erectile Disorder/Female Dyspareunia/Male Dyspareunia/ Other Female Sexual Dysfunction/ Other Male sexual Dysfunction/Substance-Induced Sexual Dysfunction
- Paraphilias; Exhibitionism/Fetishism/Frotteurism/Pedophilia (Attracted to Male/to Female/to both/Limited to Incest/)/Sexual Masochism/Sadism/Transvestic Fetishism/Voyeurism/Paraphilia NOS
- Gender Identity Disorder; NOS
- Sexual Disorder NOS
- Eating Disorders; Anorexia Nervosa/Bulimia Nervosa/NOS
- Sleep Disorders
- Dyssomnias (Primary Insomnia/Primary Hypersomnia/Narcolepsy/ Breathing Related Sleep Disorder/Circadian Rhythm Sleep Disorder/NOS
- Parasomnias; Nightmare Disorder/Sleep Terror Disorder/Sleep walking Disorder/NOS
- Sleep Disorders Related to Another Mental Disorder
- Sleep Disorders Due to General Medical Condition
- Substance Induced Sleep Disorder
- Impulse-Control Disorders; Intermittent Explosive Disorder/Kleptomania/Pathological Gambling/Trichotillmania/ Impulse Control Disorder NOS
- Malingering
- Child or Adolescent Antisocial Behavior
- Borderline Intellectual Functioning (IQ 70-90)
- Age Relative Cognitive Decline
- Bereavement

- Adjustment Disorders; With Depressed Mood/With Anxiety/Both/With Disturbance of Conduct/Mixed Disturbance of Emotions and Conduct/Unspecified
- Personality Disorders; Paranoid Personality /Schizoid/ Schizotypal/ Antisocial /Borderline/ Histrionic/ Narcissistic/Avoidant /Dependent/ Obsessive-Compulsive/ NOS
- Psychological Factors Affecting Medical Condition; Mental disorder affecting Medical Condition/Psychological Symptoms Affecting Medical Condition/Personality Traits Or Coping Style Affecting Medical Condition/Maladaptive Health Behaviors Affecting Medical Condition/Stress related Physiological Response Affecting Medical Condition/Other or Unspecified Psychological Factors Affecting Medical Condition
- Medication Induced Movement Disorder; Neuroleptic Induced Parkinsonianism/Malignant Syndrome/Acute Dystonia/Tardive Dyskinesia/Postural Tremor/NOS Movement Disorder
- Adverse Effects of Medication NOS
- Relational Problems; Related to a Mental Disorder or General Medical Condition/Parent Child problem/ Partner Problem/ Sibling Problem/ Relational Problem NOS
- Problems Related to Abuse or Neglect; Physical Abuse of Child/Sexual Abuse of Child/Neglect of Child/Physical Abuse of Adult/Sexual Abuse of Adult
- Additional Conditions That May be a Focus of Clinical Attention
- Noncompliance with Treatment
- Academic Problem
- Occupational Problem
- Identity Problem
- Religious or Spiritual Problem
- Acculturation Problem
- Phase of Life Problem

List of Other problem Behaviors which need mention
- Pyromania-Fire setting Behavior
- Erotomania-Sexual fixation on specific person
- Cultural (Cross) Shock and adjustment Difficulties
- Religious Fanaticism-Believing that people of other faith should be killed, converted, made to suffer, etc.
- Pathological Nationalism-Belief that other nationalities. ethnic groups are inferior, undeserving
- Chauvinism-Believing that people of other gender are inferior and should be socio-Politically/economically deprived.

Neurological Problems

Neurological problems present a very difficult challenge because they are difficult to diagnose, mimic many other diseases, and treatments options are rather limited. Unfortunately, many Primary Care Physicians, specialists, and schools do not fully utilize neurological consultations. Ideally, your PCP, psychologist, and school nurse should be able to understand when a neurologist consultation is indicated.

The following is a brief list of some neurological disorders. Provided they are not due to substance abuse, typical symptoms include confusion, disorientation, speech impairment, high distractibility, agitation and hyper-stimulation, inappropriate verbalizations, difficulty with memory and recall, no response to touch or sound, pain or sight, inconsistent response to commands, aggressive, bizarre, non-purposeful behavior, and short attention span.

- Frontal Lobe Dysfunctions/damage/epilepsy
- Epilepsy
- Cerebro-vascular Accident (stroke)
- Aphasia, memory deficits, intoxication, attention disorders also have neurology correlates.
- Toxicity (metals, chemicals, overdose, etc.)

Problems of very young children

- Childhood depression
- Encoprosis
- Enuresis
- Bed-wetting
- Temper Tantrums
- Acting out around meal time
- Acting out while socializing or in the shopping malls.
- Restlessness while confined in the car for long distance driving
- Excessive fears/shyness, avoidance
- Problem behavior around bedtime/sleep

References

American Psychiatric Association.(2000). Diagnostic and statistical manual of mental disorders (4th ed.,text rev.). Washington, DC: Auth.

Baumann, M., Luchesi, B., & Wilke, A. (2003). Tempel und Tamilen in zweiter Heimat: Hindus aus Sri Lanka im deutschsprachigen und skandinavischen Raum. Würzburg: Ergon.

Bates, C. (2001). Community, empire, and migration: South Asians in Diaspora. New York, N.Y.: PALGRAVE.

Bean, R., & Titus, G. (2011). Cultural Intersection of Asian Indian Ethnicity and Presenting Problem: Adapting Multicultural Competence for Clinical Accessibility. *Journal of Multicultural Counseling and Development,* 40-51.

Bhatia, S. (2007). American karma race, culture, and identity in the Indian diaspora. New York: New York University Press.

Bhattacharya, G. (1998). Drug use among Asian-Indian adolescents: Identifying protective/risk factors. *Adolescence, 33*(129), 169-184.

Bhattacharya, G. (2002). Drug Abuse Risks for Acculturating Immigrant Adolescents: Case Study of Asian Indians in the United States. *Health & Social Work,* 175-183.

Caplan, L. (2001). Children of colonialism Anglo-Indians in a postcolonial world. Oxford: Berg.

Coward, H. (2000). The South Asian religious diaspora in Britain, Canada, and the United States. Albany, NY: SUNY Press.

Dasgupta, S. (2007). *Body evidence intimate violence against South Asian women in America.* New Brunswick, N.J.: Rutgers Univ Press.

Desjarlais, R., Eisenberg, L., Good, B., & Kleinman, A. (1995). *World mental health: Problems, and priorities in low-income countries.* New York: Oxford University Press.

Dhingra, P. (2007). Managing multicultural lives Asian American professionals and the challenge of multiple identities. Stanford, Calif.: Stanford University Press.

House, A. (1999). *DSM-IV diagnosis in the schools.* New York: Guilford Press.

Mahabir, K. (1992). East indian women of Trinidad and Tobago: an annotated bibliography with photographs and ephemera. San Juan: Chakra publishing house.

Mahabir, K. (1985). The Still cry: *Personal accounts of East Indians in Trinidad and Tobago during indentureship,* 1845-1917. Tacarigua, Trinidad: Calaloux Publications.

Portman, T. A. (2001). Sex role attributions of American Indian women. *Journal of Mental Health Counseling,* 23, 72-84.

Puwar, N., Raghuram, P. (2003). *South Asian women in the diaspora.* Oxford: Berg.

Safran, W. (2005). The Jewish Diaspora in a Comparative and Theoretical Perspective. *Israel Studies, 10*(1), 36-60.

Singh, D., & Maharaj, R. (2006). *Doon Pandit: His life and times (1900-1958).* Chaguanas, Trinidad: Indian Review Press.

Sookdeo, N. (2000). Freedom, festivals and caste in Trinidad after slavery: A society in transition. USA: Xlibris Corporation.

Snyder, P., Nussbaum, P., & Robins, D. (1998). *Clinical neuropsychology: A pocket handbook for assessment.* Washington, DC: American Psychological Association.

Sundberg, N. D., Rohila, P. K., & Tyler, L. E. (1970). Values of Indian and American adolescents. Journal of Personality and Social Psychology, 16(3), 374.

Warren, M. (2001). Behavioral management guide: Essential treatment strategies for adult psychotherapy. Northvale, NJ: Jason Aronson.

Jacobsen, K. A. (2004). *South Asians in the diaspora: histories and religious traditions*, Knut A. Jacobsen and P. Pratap Kumar. Brill.

Vertovec, S. (2000). *The Hindu diaspora: Comparative patterns.* London: Routledge

Raleigh, V., Bulusu, L., & Balarajan, R. (1990). Suicides among immigrants from the Indian subcontinent. *The British Journal of Psychiatry,* 46-50.

Rukmani, T. (1999). *Hindu diaspora: Global perspectives* (1. publ. ed.). Montreal: Concordia University.

Williams, R. (1996). A Sacred thread: Modern transmission of Hindu traditions in India and abroad. New York, NY: Columbia University Press.

Vertovec, S. (1991). *Aspects of the South Asian diaspora*. Delhi: Oxford University Press.

Witkin, H., & Berry, J. (1975). Psychological differentiation in cross-cultural perspective. *Journal of Cross-cultural Psychology*.

Additional Article References

Saran, P. (1980). Patterns of Adaptation of Indian Immigrants: Challenges and Strategies. In *Uprooting and development: Dilemmas of coping with modernization* (Vol. V, pp. 375-399). Springer.

Hodge, D. (n.d.). Working with Hindu Clients in a Spiritually Sensitive Manner. *Social Work,* 27-38.

Desjarlais, R., Eisenberg, L., Good, B., & Kleinman, A. (1995). *World mental health: Problems, and priorities in low-income countries*. New York: Oxford University Press.

Lindner, Evelin G. Humiliation or Dignity: Regional Conflicts in the Global Village. Journal of Mental Health, Psychosocial work and Counseling in areas of Armed conflict, forthcoming (2002).

Varma, P. (2010). Becoming Indian: The unfinished revolution of culture and identity. *New Delhi: Allen Lane, Penguin Books.*

Web References

Global Hindu Diaspora - A bibliography of books and main articles. https://www.unilu.ch/fileadmin/shared/Publikationen/baumann_global-hindu-diaspora.pdf

Shah, B., & Kumar, N. (2005, January 1). Mental Health Research in India (Technical Monograph on ICMR Mental Health Studies). Retrieved from http://www.icmr.nic.in/publ/Mental Helth .pdf

Pravasi Bharatiya Divas – Engaging the Diaspora: The Way Forward. (n.d.). http://moia.gov.in/writereaddata/pdf/proceedings_2010.pdf

Anjum, Z. (2006, November 12). An Ode to the Indian Diaspora. http://www.littleindia.com/nri/1388-an-ode-to-the-indian-Diaspora.Html

Kapur, A. (2012, March 10). How India Became America. Retrieved from http://www.nytimes.com/2012/03/11/opinion/sunday/how-india-became-america.html?Pagewanted=all

Trishanku. (n.d.). http://en.wikipedia.org/wiki/Trishanku

Human Rights Reports. (n.d.). Retrieved from http://www.hafsite.org/resources/human_rights_report

India among countries with highest number of HIV adolescents http://www.isidelhi.org.in/hrnews/HR_THEMATIC_ISSUES/Health/Health-2011.pdf

India Tribune. (n.d.). Retrieved from http://www.indiatribune.com/index.php?option=com_content&view=article&id=7286:15-commit-suicide-every-hour-in-india-majority-victims-married-report&catid=125:general-news&Itemid=400

'Over 5K children raped, another 1,408 murdered in 2010' - The Times of India. (n.d.). Retrieved February 8, 2015, from http://articles.timesofindia.indiatimes.com/2011-10-30/india/30338511_1_cases-of-sexual-assault-uttar-pradesh-madhya-pradesh

Dube, K., Kumar, A., & Dube, S. (n.d.). Psychiatric training and therapies in Ayurved. Retrieved from http://psycnet.apa.org/psycinfo/1986-18361-001

Personality types in Ayurveda. (n.d.). Retrieved February 8, 2015, from http://psycnet.apa.org/psycinfo/1984-31446-001

Kapur, R., & Chandrashekar, C. (n.d.). Extension of mental health service through psychiatric camps: A new approach. Retrieved from http://repository.ias.ac.in/31108/

Kumar, S. (n.d.). IPI — Indian thought and tradition: A psychohistorical perspective. Retrieved from http://ipi.org.in/texts/kirankumar/kk-ip-history.php

Faulkner, J. (2005). Freud's Concept of the Death Drive and its Relation to the Superego. http://www.minerva.mic.ul.ie/vol9/freud.html

www.ingramcontent.com/pod-product-compliance
Lightning Source LLC
Chambersburg PA
CBHW071534040426
42452CB00008B/1017